For One Another
Touching Hearts in a Changing World

by

Kenneth Kremer

Northwestern Publishing House
Milwaukee, Wisconsin

Library of Congress Control Number: 2001132673
Northwestern Publishing House
1250 N. 113th St., Milwaukee, WI 53226-3284
http://www.nph.net
© 2001 Northwestern Publishing House
Published 2001
Printed in the United States of America
ISBN 0-8100-1361-4

To Nancy: 7-21-02

As a dear sister and friend
in Christ, I admire the
compassion you have
for others. May this
book encourage you
to continue to use your
gifts for His glory!

To Marlis —

my excellent model of

Christian compassion

Love
and
prayers,
Deb

Let your light shine before men,
that they may see your good deeds
and praise your Father in heaven.

Matthew 5:16

CONTENTS

PREFACE

In the fifties, when I was growing up, believers and unbelievers looked the same. The Bible says we should be able to
tell the difference by the fruit people produce in their lives.
But back then it was hard to distinguish between the actions
of believers and unbelievers. Everyone helped neighbors or
offered assistance when someone was in trouble. And no one
talked religion outside of church or the home. At least they
didn't in my neighborhood. It was considered rude. So we seldom knew where neighbors stood on moral issues or matters
of faith. Maybe people were just more reserved about their
personal convictions a half-century ago. Or maybe the unbelievers of the world sensed the demise of the Judeo-Christian
culture and were content to wait a little longer before they
brought out the fruit that was slowly ripening in the private
pantries of their hearts.

Of course, I saw it only from a child's perspective. But the
contrast between then and now can be instructive. Whether or
not our culture has been in steady decline over the last century

is still a subject of hot debate. Secular historians argue that open and tolerant attitudes stimulate religious interest. Christians, on the other hand, see contemporary culture as awash in dishonesty and immorality. We witness this moral degradation in the political arena, in business, in the media, even in education. We are affected by it. Some of us are getting caught up in it. Our families are being reshaped by it. So are our churches.

The Western world is in the process of rejecting its Judeo-Christian roots. Gays and lesbians are out of the closet with their full-fledged, in-your-face politics. Pro-choice activists face off daily against pro-life advocates in our nation's courts and in the media. Sexual immorality is practiced in open defiance of God's prohibition of fornication and adultery. Divine authority and biblical truth are ridiculed as passé. God's moral law does not align with the secular notion that circumstances at the moment determine what is right or wrong.

Great changes are taking place in the world. And a lot more is involved than the usual passing of the torch from one generation to the next. People think in ways that are different than the ways people thought a generation ago—different in ways that sometimes seem to defy reason. The previous generation took for granted that truth could be discovered, though many members of the generation looked for truth in the wrong places. Today people doubt that truth can exist, or if it does, they postulate that it is different for each of us. Instinct and intuition are given more credence than logic and rational thinking. Communication styles have sustained substantial setbacks, not just in how we talk with one another but in the actual things we say to each other and in the way we hear others speaking to us. The way we group ourselves socially no longer resembles the social groupings of just a generation ago. A tribal order with cultlike dynamics threatens to dismantle the institution of the family. Leadership styles are undergoing a major revolution. The paradigms for generating new ideas and for making important decisions are radically new. Entrepreneurial risk is being traded in favor of managed risk, based on mathematical probabilities.

Some would have us believe that this intellectual transformation is all about an explosion of new technology—the Internet or virtual reality—or that it is the result of discoveries like those made through the Human Genome Project. It isn't. It isn't just another movement either, toward a world bank or a global economy. Nor is it just a cultural phenomenon—a new level of the hurried lifestyle—or the result of the media's influence, multiculturalism, or reurbanization. It isn't the result of another wrinkle in Einsteinian particle-theory physics or a string-theory view of the universe. It isn't Darwin, Nietzsche, or Freud revisited. It isn't a resurgence of nihilism, existentialism, relativism, materialism, humanism or a half dozen other isms. This transformation of thought encompasses more than all these phenomena and movements and isms combined. As we take our first steps into a new millennium, we find ourselves in a world that, in many ways, defies definition.

Whatever name one chooses to give this philosophy that grips the world today, and however we define it, we are living in a world turned upside down with revolutionary ideas—human ideas, secular ideas—some of them perhaps not as new as we might think. The upshot of it all is that the potential for a dynamic and volatile future is quickly slipping into the present. And just about everything we have become comfortable with in our lifetimes is suddenly under suspicion.

That the cumulative effect of these changes is dramatic is an understatement. We appear to be standing on the threshold of a whole new epoch in human history. Though we may not be able to agree on what to call it or how to measure it, define it, or analyze it, we still need to discuss what these changes mean. God's people, both individually and collectively, have a vital stake in grappling with this generation's new way of looking at the universe. Sensitivity to these changes is critical to our gospel ministry.

In these times, ought we to feel threatened? Or will we be surprised to find the future filled to overflowing with opportunities to evangelize many more lost souls for eternity? Whatever the case, we cannot afford to ignore what is going on around us, hoping that these dramatic changes are just a passing fad. Unless we take the time to consider the spiritual landscape in which we stand, we may exhaust ourselves wandering in confusion and miss many opportunities for Christian witness.

On the other hand, we need to take care that we not become transfixed by these changes. For then we would lose sight of our mission. Whatever becomes of this changing world, we can be certain of two things. First, as always, God is in control. As always, his purposes will be met as he turns evil for the good of his people. He will judge the wicked. And he will provide the strength we need to stand and advance, even when we are assaulted by the very gates of hell. Second, our future in heaven is safe. Our faith rests on the hope we have in Jesus' own promises to bring us to his Father's eternal home. None of that has changed, is changing, or will change in the future. Secure in that hope, the time we spend anticipating his return can be productive. Because we want to be productive, we become students of the times, studying the ways people think, the reasons they do what they do, the languages they speak, not just for our own benefit — but *for one another*.

The concept of the Christian life-focus *for one another* is neither new nor of human origin. Phrases drawn from the epistles, such as *encourage one another; spur one another on; speak to one another in psalms, hymns, and spiritual songs; instruct one another; accept one another; honor one another,* serve nicely as a framework for defining the Christian life of sanctification. Ten such New Testament expressions are included in this collection, though Scripture suggests more. The concept has its origins in the writings of the Old Testament. In Ecclesiastes 11:1, for example, God encourages his people, "Cast your bread upon the waters." Using the picture of a farmer taking some of his precious grain to use as seed, with the hope of a harvest, the inspired teacher instructs us to use what we have to benefit others — with the hope of another kind of harvest.

The gospel changes us, marks us as Christ's own, and sets us apart from the rest of the world — to serve only him. Our desire is to live, as Martin Luther put it, like *little Christs*. That desire grows in the heart that grasps the message of the cross and in which the Spirit of Christ dwells. Surely the message of the cross serves as the headwaters for every Christian's life. From those headwaters flow acts of service, kindness, and compassion, as Jesus lives *in us*, who first understand what Jesus has done *for us*.

The Christian's eye of faith is always focused on what Christ has done *for us*. God's Word shows us Jesus' sacrifice on the cross *for us*. Baptism offers a daily reminder of Jesus *for us*. Weekly sermons in church proclaim Jesus *for us*. The Holy Supper offers his body and blood given *for us*. Jesus *for us* is the good news; we call it the gospel. The Holy Spirit uses this gospel in the Word and sacrament to plant and nurture the seed of faith in our hearts. What follows is about the impact a Christian's faith has in the here and now as Christ lives *in us*. It is a call to remember that our mission remains the same even in a changing world. The purpose of this book is to challenge every Christian to look into the mirror and be objective about how well we are carrying out Jesus' Great Commission in our present setting. It is about bearing fruit as we enter the new millennium into which God has placed us.

These changing times challenge us to step out of our passive church mode so that God's voice is amplified in our everyday lives. Our words and our actions may offend the secular city, but we can no longer give in to the myth that confines faith life to our homes and churches. As unbelievers watch us, some will discover Jesus. In many cases they will be drawn to him by what they see in the way we treat one another . . . and them. At first they will see Christ's love in action. Eventually they will see the author of that love, and they will experience the transcendent hope and peace that Christ alone offers.

How you and I love our neighbors in today's changing world is directly connected to the way in which Jesus conducted his ministry on earth. He healed the sick, restored sight to the blind, and shed tears of sorrow for the dead. He listened. He hurt when others hurt. He had compassion on the sick, the forgotten, the dying, the lonely. He was outspoken in urging us to follow suit. He wants us to be salt and light to a world rotting in sin and perishing in darkness, to offer a cup of cold water, give up our cloaks, visit the imprisoned, and feed the hungry. "Love each other as I have loved you" (John 15:12).

God's will for us today is the same as it was for first-century Christians. "Love your neighbor as yourself," wrote the apostle Paul. Then he added, "And do this, *understanding the present time*" (Romans 13:9,11).

The present time is truly extraordinary. And for it God provides extraordinary people to carry out his work in the most ordinary of circumstances. Jesus nurtures us so that we might be such people, distinguished from the rest of the world by our fruit. Of such individuals Jesus himself said, "By this all men will know that you are my disciples, if you love one another" (John 13:35).

In your lifetime it is quite likely that someone has reached out to you with this love. Perhaps the parents who brought you to your baptism, the spouse who patiently endured your skepticism and spoke out of love, or the friend who loved you when no one else would. Such individuals are worth remembering and celebrating. But there are others living in our time who still need attention. There is still a need to live for one another. That challenge is worth exploring.

ACKNOWLEDGMENTS

One of the great wonders in life is that all our stories are so similar. We are conceived. Nine months later we pass through our mothers' birth canals and draw our first breaths. We learn. We grow to adulthood. We work. We engage in creative endeavors. We love. We interact. Some of us marry. Some of us bear children. A few of us make a mark in life big enough to be remembered for a generation or two. And then we die. The stencil of life is reused over and over. And yet, in all this sameness, each of our stories is a profoundly different saga, distinctive, unique from every other individual's personal adventure. This book celebrates that remarkable diversity. So I am deeply indebted to those who shared their odysseys. Without your stories, this book could never have been written.

I am also most grateful to the many friends and colleagues who offered criticism as the manuscript progressed through its various stages. Your honest reactions helped me maintain focus. Your encouragement kept me on task. Thank you.

Finally, I would be remiss if I failed to mention the contributions of Marlis, my partner in life. Most of what I know about godly compassion, I learned from her. That knowledge has proven to be a gift of incalculable value—a treasure beyond measure. Over the years I have come to realize that there is no way to repay someone for such a gift. You simply accept it with thanks and put it to work. What follows represents my feeble attempt to pay a long overdue tribute to her by putting her gift to work in the form of this book.

KJK

This is how we know what love is:

Jesus Christ laid down his life for us.

1 John 3:16

CHAPTER ONE

THE BATTLEFIELD

My earliest memories were shaped by war. In 1944 my father landed on a beachhead near Cherbourg, France. For the next year he, along with thousands of other American GIs, fought his way to Berlin. When the war was over, Europe was in shambles, but the world of my life remained safe and secure.

My brothers and sister and I never tired of hearing my father's stories. We sat for hours, admiring his war memorabilia—medals, pictures, uniform insignia, maps, and newspaper clippings. One snapshot, in particular, remains etched in my memory. In it, my hero is dressed in full battle gear, posing in a foxhole. The ominous landscape insinuates the horrors of war and reminds me that many fathers didn't come home to their families.

My father put his life on the line for his family and friends. But he also did it for strangers. Knowing that my father was one of those brave soldiers willing to sacrifice their lives in that cause still swells my heart with pride. They were prepared to die, and many of them did, so that we would continue to be free.

My father's actions reflected his faith—he was a living example of something Jesus once said to his disciples: "Greater love has no one than this, that he lay down his life for his friends" (John 15:13). My dad was willing to do just that.

World War II and my father's willingness to sacrifice are humble, perhaps even feeble, illustrations of a much greater war and an even greater sacrifice. Christ's victory over sin, death, and Satan at Calvary is forever. You and I are the beneficiaries of all Christ did. Extravagant as the price was, Christ's great sacrifice gave us life and eternal freedom from the prospect of a spiritual holocaust, suffered in the confines of a very real hell. Christ left the glory of heaven and experienced injustice of cosmic proportions. He suffered his Father's devastating wrath, bore the burden of untold shame, endured excruciating physical and psychological pain, and died, all *for us*—sinners. In return we can do little more than thank him for the life-giving sacrifice and live in grateful service to him.

This is where the biblical concept of *for one another* begins. "This is how God showed his love among us: He sent his one and only Son into the world that we might live through him. This is love: not that we loved God, but that he loved us and sent his Son as an atoning sacrifice for our sins" (1 John 4:9,10).

The noble story of the cross is the only story that matters to our eternal salvation. But it is not the whole story. Now God's love for us works its way into our human relationships. "We love because he first loved us. If anyone says, 'I love God,' yet hates his brother, he is a liar. For anyone who does not love his brother, whom he has seen, cannot love God, whom he has not seen" (1 John 4:19,20).

We love others because he first loved us. We read this in our Bibles. Jesus' love for us is compelling. His love for us demands a response.

To the unbelieving world, loving one another is altruistic claptrap. People who don't know Jesus have never experienced his selfless, forgiving love in their own lives. They cannot imagine it. Our sinful natures have inherited the unbeliever's view of love—the self-absorbed, self-directed, self-interested response to the things that please us. But Jesus loves us in spite of ourselves, loves us so much that he died to cleanse us of the guilt our self-centered love has brought upon us. Love that spawned such sacrifice drives us to love; it moves us; it motivates us. It is the dynamic that gives purpose and meaning to our lives.

But what is this love? What kind of attitudes are loving attitudes? What kind of behaviors demonstrate love? What are love's goals and objectives? Would-be lovers wrestle with such questions.

My grandchildren climb onto my lap, wrap their arms around my neck, and hug me with so much affection that I'm overwhelmed with joy. As though they want the whole world to hear, they declare, "Grandpa, I love you." Then one pipes up, "Grandpa, can you read me a story?" Life doesn't get any better. And, in many ways, love doesn't get much more concrete than that. Their words, in combination with their attitudes and actions, demonstrate a love that would otherwise remain in the realm of theory and conjecture.

Children have little concern for theories. As short as their lives have been, my grandchildren have learned to recognize the love of their parents and grandparents. The desire to sit in my lap, the hugs, and the words are all part of a complete package that proclaims, in no uncertain terms, "I love you."

That is how love works. Love is more than a word; it is an attitude inexorably connected to actions. Such love is never completely idle or at rest. Love—godly love—is a faith-generated response to the love Jesus has shown us. Christians are not just *in love* with the rest of the people who share this planet; we are in hot pursuit of every opportunity to do those loving things that distinguish us as followers of Jesus. We learn what biblical love is by observing God in action throughout history. And we practice biblical love by participating in the lifelong adventure of reflecting God's love to others.

Saint Paul said, "Love never fails" (1 Corinthians 13:8). And he provided a list of ways to show others that we love them. "Love is patient, love is kind. It does not envy, it does not boast, it is not proud. It is not rude, it is not self-seeking, it is not easily angered, it keeps no record of wrongs. Love does not delight in evil but rejoices with the truth. It always protects, always trusts, always hopes, always perseveres." And a few verses later, Paul added this powerful statement regarding Christian love: "Now these three remain: faith, hope and love. But the greatest of these is love" (1 Corinthians 13:4-7,13).

The apostle John (sometimes referred to as the Apostle of Love) tells us that "God *is* love" (1 John 4:16). What a stunning revelation about the nature of our God! With three words John has probed a deep, eternal mystery. They tell us volumes about love's origin and power. At the heart of this broad truth

4

is the simple concept that God doesn't just act out of love or demonstrate his love, *he embodies it.* This is one of those biblical concepts that may be easy to say but that no human mind (since the fall) can fully grasp. As ideas go, it is just that big. So, in faith, we trust this to be true.

"Of course," one might argue, "God is a spirit. He doesn't have a body. When we say *God embodies love,* we are using figurative language." Ah, but it was in bodily form that God's love was most clearly revealed to us. He came into the world of sin in bodily form. And that was hardly a figure of speech. It was a real event in human history. He really lived here, in the flesh, among us sinners. He suffered, as we suffer. He died, as we die. Christ Jesus is the very embodiment of God's love for mankind. His life-giving words, his humble attitude, his selfless behavior, and his sacrificial actions all flowed from the heart of his Father's superactive love for us. That love is observable and on the record. And that record (the Bible) stands throughout all times and for all people as a testimony to God's transcendent love for us.

You and I need to review the record of God's love often. But we must be careful not to tell and retell God's love story as though it were over and done—a thing of the past. Our redemption is complete, but his love story is a living history that extends from the past to the present and into the future. Furthermore, it involves us, not just as its grateful recipients but as vessels through which God carries his love to others— we are God's designated lovers, reaching out to a changing world. The Apostle of Love put it like this: "Whoever lives in love lives in God, and God in him" (1 John 4:16). John is speaking about us. He is saying that, by virtue of our faith in

Jesus, we are fully capable of loving others—even those who, to our sinful natures, seem unlovable.

Letti is one of those vessels who carry God's love to others— an extraordinary person whom God has placed into ordinary circumstances. A widow and not always in the best health, Letti rarely lets her own frailty get in the way of her mission, which is to love others in whatever way she can. On Sunday mornings she brings several mentally impaired people to church. She talks their language, explaining things in a gentle voice. During the service Letti holds a hymnal open for a young woman with Down's syndrome who wants to give her very best efforts to the singing. As the members come forward for Communion, Letti steadies an elderly, hearing-impaired lady at the railing so that she can receive the Lord's Supper with the rest of the congregation. Then, back in the pew, Letti clasps the hands of a child in hers while the congregation prays. After the service Letti makes a point of talking to a lonely member who has been suffering from depression. Then she offers a ride home to a stranded teen.

During the week Letti writes notes to people who are awaiting test results from the hospital or who are about to undergo surgery. Periodically she visits a member who rarely gets out of the house because she lives in mortal fear of falling.

Letti also participates in a weekly prayer circle. She joins other women in the congregation who come together to pray for members and nonmembers in need of special prayers.

You can see Jesus working in Letti . . . and through her. It's a beautiful sight—love in motion. The members of our church don't spend much time thinking about definitions of love or theorizing about the nature of Christian compassion. With people like Letti around, who needs definitions or theories?

Our churches have many Lettis in them—people imprinted with the love of their Lord Jesus, inflamed with an eternal mission. Their love for others extends far beyond their words; they live it. In them you and I can see Christ's love taking wing. And we can celebrate their heroic spirit by emulating them in our own lives.

Accept one another, then, just as Christ accepted you, in order to bring praise to God.

Romans 15:7

CHAPTER TWO

THE CLUBHOUSE

In the early fifties, Milwaukee's near north-side was popu-
lated mostly by Caucasians. It wasn't until later in that same
decade that our neighborhood became racially integrated. So
being of white European extract wasn't an issue yet. Nor was
nationality or ethnicity. We were the stew simmering in the so-
called American melting pot—the sons, grandsons, and great-
grandsons of one European migration after another—Poles, old
Germans, new Germans, Irish, Serbs, Slavs, Jews.

Still, at age 9 or 10, even little boys have their prejudices. In
the case of our little neighborhood gang, gender tested the limits of our tolerance. Members of the fairer sex didn't see life the
same way little boys saw it. (Not that we really cared.) Girls
couldn't run like boys. They didn't appreciate dirt or worms or
snakes as we did. And what was the big problem with sweat?
This much we knew: these creatures were different from us.
We were paranoid; anyone who was different must surely be
plotting against us.

And the paranoia didn't stop with gender. Any outsiders—including adults—were suspect in general, just because they were outsiders. So we constructed barriers against them. We created our own identity and a subculture that would insulate us and protect us from outsiders and the unknown dangers they might bring.

In the fifties, a nine-year-old's favorite barrier against outsiders was a clubhouse. The old tin garage at the back of our lot was a fine example. In its prime it was furnished with a frayed Persian carpet remnant from a nearby wholesale house, a wooden chair with one leg shorter than the others, and a small rolltop desk, painted baby blue. During summer heat waves, the air inside was stifling. The tiny windows in the back didn't open more than an inch or two. Their frosted glass panels were embedded with chicken wire. They were impossible to break and just as impossible to see through. Perfect! Security was a high priority for little-boy nonsense.

Anyone allowed to enter had to go through the initiation ritual, which consisted of taking a sacred oath and commingling blood. Our brotherhood was tight; we even had a secret signal. (This was the age of decoder rings and Buck Rogers technology.) The signal could only be produced by holding a privet hedge leaf tightly between the heels of one's thumbs and blowing gently: "Thweeeeeet!" Only that uncommon sound permitted passage beyond the club's double-locked tin door.

Today, in my life and in the lives of the people around me, I see ghosts of my own childhood. This clubhouse mentality germinated quite innocently in the soil of childhood fantasy.

We imagined threats to our security. We instinctively sought ways to ensure our self-preservation and combat our paranoia. *Different* meant dangerous, even if the perceived danger was only make-believe.

The adult world, however, takes these differences quite seriously. And we act on our instincts in the way we make social choices and in the way we join, or reject, the people around us. We carefully choose the neighborhoods we live in. For many of us, that choice is based on social, racial, ethnic, or economic criteria. Where we live often sends others a loud message regarding our financial success or our status in the community. Living in the wrong place or associating with the wrong people can threaten our image.

Image is very important today. From childhood on we are seduced to play the social games that generate a certain image in the eyes of the world. We call it our *identity*. Others will judge us, based on their early impressions. Opportunities will be won or lost by the images we project. Our choices in clothes, our style of communication (laid back, fiercely competitive, flip, coy, intellectual, careful), our work ethic, the people we spend time with, the restaurants we frequent, the entertainment we seek—all work together to project an image that is vitally important if we want to be somebody in today's world. We codify the things we say so that insiders will get it and outsiders won't. Our body language tells people when we are confident in our surroundings and when we are not. More than anything else, our carefully constructed identity says (to us even more loudly than to others) *I belong.*

We also make statements about perceived differences by the ways in which we choose our associates. Some of us use memberships in local country clubs, service organizations, or professional associations to formalize our sense of belonging. We may even choose a church in this way. Most of us identify with people of our own culture, our own age, our own stage in life. We confide in members of our own gender and prefer to be grouped with people who share a similar vocation in life. We are profoundly class conscious.

Some of this is healthy. These associations (subcultures) make us feel safe and comfortable. They help us fit in. They connect us to one another, giving us a sense of togetherness and community.

But because of the corrosive effects of sin, there is also a downside to cultural identity. These subcultures we construct can, and often do, isolate us from the rest of the world. Some are even designed to do just that. And they can set us against others in ways that are, in fact, antisocial.

Take, for example, the swirl of tensions seething just below the surface in many junior and senior high schools today. At this age students operate in a world of oversimplified characterizations: Geeks, Nerds, Preppies, Jocks, Ghettoes, Gothics, Greasers, and the like. The labels have multiplied over the years. The rivalry and animosity between groups is sometimes intense. Almost every young person's perception of self is linked to a peer-group image. The individual is subordinate to the whims of the group. Young people today don't place a high premium on the value of the individual. Nor do they seek direction from the wisest or the most visionary leaders in their group. Instead, an opinion, based on a consensus at any given time, will prevail. Without rhyme or reason, the group will change direction like a school of fishes in perfect rhythm with one another.

The term *tribal* has been used to describe this kind of behavior. This tribal mind-set has been recognized as a significant factor in several of the tragic, Columbine-type incidents on school campuses. Even more frightening, this mind-set has become widespread and thus establishes a troubling new cultic view of social interaction for the next generation of adults.

As effective as these subcultures are in making us feel part of a group, are they also effective in slamming the door to outsiders.

The Great Commission is aimed at opening doors, not slamming them shut. If the objective is to reach out to those who still don't know Jesus as their Savior, practicing social exclusivity is hardly the way to do it. Membership should never depend on being a certain color or having the right genetic code. It doesn't have anything to do with gender. Older people are no more or less eligible for membership in God's kingdom than the young. The size of a person's stock portfolio or bank account isn't a factor. Among God's people there is no place for clandestine handshakes, secret codes, inner loops, or self-styled cliques.

Some of our churches are better at welcoming outsiders than others. Not long ago, my wife and I took an autumn weekend getaway to Wisconsin's north country. The local newspaper advertised a harvest celebration scheduled for that same weekend. It was sponsored by a Lutheran church. The Harvestfest sounded like a good way to get a sense of what the community was like. We had to eat anyway; so we went.

The event was obviously a highlight of the year for the members of this congregation. Freshly cut flowers and tall candlesticks adorned each of the linen-covered tables. The food looked superb and smelled delicious: turkey, mashed potatoes and gravy, candied sweet potatoes, cranberries . . .

It was a sit-down event. Kids from the church's teen group, decked out in their finest suits and dresses, waited on tables. People scurried in and out of the tiny kitchen with serving trays and bowls heaped with food. Everyone was enjoying the fellowship and the ambiance. My wife and I took the last two empty chairs at a table filled with happy faces. The prayer came first; then "Pass the potatoes, please."

When we're among strangers, my wife usually does better at making first contact. She took the lead, broaching several conversational opportunities with her neighbors. Nothing. I noted her failure and decided to attempt a conversation with an older gent sitting to my left: "Wonderful meal." Nothing. "Does your church do this every year?" Still nothing. I turned to the young mom sitting across from me. A nonthreatening question about her son, who was sitting next to her, might elicit a friendly response. Or so I thought. Nothing.

It's usually quite easy to begin a conversation with teens. My wife tried a light-hearted quip about decaf coffee, aimed at getting a response from the girl serving coffee. Nothing. In just a few minutes, we had gotten the message: This was hostile territory. We didn't belong. It had nothing to do with any of the usual racial, economic, or ethnic barriers. We were outsiders.

We wolfed down our food and left the hall as quickly as we could. On the way out, I decided that common courtesy required us to seek out the pastor and offer a friendly greeting. In this way, I reasoned, we might still salvage something of our experience and perhaps leave on a warmer note. We found the pastor in the parish office. Putting on our best smiles, we introduced ourselves and mentioned how impressive the church building was. Nothing. Worse, he gave us the proverbial cold shoulder, barely extending us the courtesy of looking up from his computer screen to make eye contact. We didn't fit into his cultural context either. In fact, we were barely even visible on his cultural screen.

"You are all sons of God through faith in Christ Jesus," wrote Saint Paul, "for all of you who were baptized into Christ have clothed yourselves with Christ. There is neither Jew nor Greek, slave nor free, male nor female, for you are all one in Christ Jesus" (Galatians 3:26-28).

One in Christ Jesus. That phrase bears repeating. Not *one* because of culture, tradition, ethnic similarities, or even common experience. One *in Christ Jesus.* We belong to one another because of him. His life, death, resurrection, and ascension are the epoxy that fuses us together in a holy union. We come together Sunday after Sunday to join our hearts and our voices in worshiping him and to encourage one another with his Word and in his name. We share the material blessings of our livelihoods in order to carry out the work of his ministry. It is Christ who makes us one through Word and sacrament. He welds our conferences of churches, our associations, our institutions, and our church body and its districts into a unit. His body and blood, given and shed for us, bind us together in communion with him and with one another. He is our one head. His Word is our one guide. He is our one and only Savior.

Oneness already exists, but how easily we forget that. Accepting others into the inner sanctum of our lives is far more difficult than most of us are willing to admit. Oneness in Christ doesn't always fit our own self-interests. We would prefer to set up our own rules to determine who belongs in our loop and who must remain on the periphery.

As a Lutheran school administrator, I occasionally heard parents admit to wanting parochial education for their child so that they wouldn't have to deal with the riffraff in public schools. They feared that someone else's wayward kids would be passing out joints on the school bus or exposing their kids to pornography. They were sadly mistaken in their assumptions about public education and parochial education. They saw our Christian school as a cultural fortress—a haven from evil—instead of a place to nurture their child's faith. I never knew how to react to that attitude. Certainly the children attending our school were far from being angels. On the other hand, from what I knew about the public system, things were hardly as bad as these parents made it seem.

Since it happened surprisingly often, I felt compelled to report the phenomenon to other leaders in the congregation. Their response was often one of righteous indignation. I was usually subtly encouraged to screen out the *hypocrites* who wanted to use our school for the wrong reason. (The board members had apparently also forgotten that we too were once riffraff in God's eyes.) I never knew how to react to their suggestion either.

God's Holy Spirit uses us to gather others in. The harvest will happen with us or without us. But it will surely happen. Sometimes it will happen in spite of our own shortcomings and prejudices. We can serve the Lord's purposes willingly or become obstacles to the gospel's free flow. We can grasp opportunities or slam the doors of our own self-righteous attitudes and clubhouse mentality in people's faces. In either case, the work will get done; God will see to that. But that will not excuse us if we have been unloving.

The apostle Paul recognized the problem. He knew that people of the same cultural background, language, and experience build walls between themselves and alien cultures. In effect, they teach one another to mistrust outsiders. But Paul also knew they had a far greater need than the security blanket of cultural identity. So he personally resolved to take on an attitude. "I have become all things to all men," he wrote, "so that by all possible means I might save some" (1 Corinthians 9:22). Paul's zeal for sharing Jesus with unbelievers didn't cool just because the people he met were different. Quite the opposite, he went the extra mile in showing that his message transcended the trappings of culture. And he did this, we are told, "for the sake of the gospel" (verse 23).

The church is indeed a refuge, but not from the unbelieving riffraff out there in our society. It is a refuge from God's anger and eternal punishment. It offers healing and reconciliation with our heavenly Father—to all.

The reconciliation and healing we share and the unity we enjoy with one another are special blessings of membership in God's family. But sometimes our social instincts so blur our vision that we miss the beauty of that oneness in Christ.

The attitude of accepting one another is an attitude fostered close to home. One subtle way in which God's people may unwittingly undermine that attitude is the disturbing way we tend to "slice and dice" church members into bite-sized ministry pieces. It is a trend that seems to be gathering momentum, especially in medium-sized and larger congregations. The strategy is apparently aimed at exploiting our natural instincts to be grouped among our peers. We plan some worship services for those who are hip to contemporary trends and other worship services for the traditionalists among us. We niche-market our organizations and Bible study programs to parents with very young children, parents of adolescents, and single moms. We isolate the elderly members in organizations for seniors. We minister to teens in their teen groups. And we subdivide our children even more. The strategy is very pragmatic and eminently popular. Everybody seems happy with this arrangement. Why? Because most of us long to be identified with our own kind. That is how we have been programmed to think.

One has to wonder just how far a trend of this kind can go without creating even more barriers and obstacles in our relationships. One has to doubt if this trend supports God's intention for establishing family units in which the wisdom of old age, the idealism of youth, and the realism of middle age can coexist side by side. In today's segmented models of churches, some of the family unity we once enjoyed seems to be slipping away. And such isolation can foster unloving attitudes. Church leaders will need to look for organizational models that unite God's people instead of fragmenting them. As we learn to cherish the unity we share in our families, we will find it easier to cherish the unity we share with other believers, even those who are different from us.

This much ought to be self-evident: we cannot love someone we refuse to accept, and we cannot accept someone we refuse to love. None of what might be considered the Christian life will matter if we are unwilling to accept others into our circle of faith.

Accepting others involves risk. We are acutely aware of the risks involved in extending an open hand of invitation to an outsider. At the very least, there is the chance we will lose face or suffer outright rejection. We risk being severely criticized by peers who are unwilling to accept those who are different. Personal honor is at stake; self-respect is on the line.

I have a neighbor who sports a "badass biker" insignia on the windshield of his Harley. It's an image he cultivates. We're talking *Outlaws* or *Hell's Angels*! He's argumentative and takes pleasure in riling up the neighborhood by flaunting his personal right to be different, even if different to him means breaking the law or being antisocial. His vocabulary is vile. So are his friends and his backyard parties. He treats his dog better than he treats his "old lady." His twin box speakers are usually cranked so loud the windows rattle. He revs his Hog in the middle of the night just to antagonize.

I walked past his house every day for years. Out of habit we ignored each other. Then, one day, I decided there was no real reason to be uncivil. So I greeted him . . . awkwardly, "Hi."

He grunted—no eye contact.

I repeated the same greeting the next day and the day after. I refused to let him ignore me.

Eventually he returned the greeting with a little jerk of his head . . . and a hint of incidental eye contact.[1]

I made small talk. "Nice pipes! Sounds like the timing's off." (That was the limit of my biker palaver.) In time we were having clumsy conversations about the weather and high property taxes. One day he took me for a wild ride around the neighborhood on his Hog. It must have been quite a sight. Eventually he turned the amplifier on his boom box down a notch or two. Now, when I'm around, he even tones down his salty language.

We are both very aware of our cultural differences, but we don't dwell on them. Nor do we try to figure each other out. Our relationship has never really been mired in social games. We look for the things we have in common. Slowly, I think, the trust between us is growing because I accept him as he is and he accepts me as I am.

Oddly, I see the two of us as being not all that different. We are both desperate people, guilty of hating God, of disobeying him, of turning our backs on him, of making war with him, of ignoring him, and of defying and denying him. We both need help. I know how badly I need a Savior, and I know where to turn for my salvation. He doesn't. That's the only real difference between us. And I am working on narrowing that gap. He is not attending church with me yet, but at least we're headed in the right direction.

Rome was the melting pot of its day, sort of like my old Brown Street neighborhood. The first Christian church in Rome had an interesting membership list. The cultural differences between its members were far more apparent than any similarities. Yet people enjoyed coming together from all walks of life and social strata to worship God with one heart and voice. Jews and Gentiles, men and women, Roman citizens and Roman subjects, freemen and slaves were not only managing to get along, they were knit together in authentic unity. And it was Christ himself who united them. What a testimony to the power of the gospel! The almighty God, who at Babel had driven a wedge between all the peoples of the world, was now reuniting them under the banner of their Lord Jesus. Even in Rome, of all places, they were, in every sense of Paul's expression, "one in Christ Jesus."

The apostle Paul prayed for that congregation: "May the God who gives endurance and encouragement give you a spirit of unity among yourselves as you follow Christ Jesus, so that with one heart and mouth you may glorify the God and Father of our Lord Jesus Christ." And he encouraged the members of this multicultural stew to foster unity in their daily lives: "Accept one another, then," he said, "just as Christ accepted you, in order to bring praise to God" (Romans 15:5-7).

The Latin Kings was the only family Sergio ever knew. His biological father together with his uncles and cousins were all members. They called themselves *gangstas*. Most of them had done time. They had participated in carjackings, thefts, armed robberies, rapes, and murders. This was all Sergio knew about life: the streets, beating the odds, avoiding police, outsmarting the system, guarding turf, *earning a living* through a life of crime. At age 8 he carried payoffs, acted as a lookout, ran messages, delivered dope, tagged boundaries, and scoped out enemy territory. By 14 he had participated in several carjackings and was involved in a drive-by shooting. A rival gang put a price on his head. Already by the age of 18, Sergio had narrowly escaped street execution several times.

Violence and death are a part of day-to-day life in "gangsta land." Statistically speaking, Sergio could not expect to live beyond his early twenties. That is the price of belonging. Sergio knew the odds. He belonged. That's all that mattered.

One night Sergio got sloppy. He was alone and failed to leave himself an escape route. Rival gangstas jumped him. Sergio took an ice pick in his face. The injury was nearly fatal, missing his eye by a fraction of an inch, his brain by a few inches.

That same night a Roman Catholic priest who had organized a local Christian gang-rehab program was riding in the police squad that responded to Sergio's clash with rival gang members. As the ambulance attendants prepared to transport Sergio's bleeding body to the hospital, the priest tucked a pamphlet beneath the gurney belt. It somehow remained with Sergio's personal belongings until he went home from the hospital. He left the pamphlet on his dresser for the next few weeks without looking at it. Then, one day, he glanced at it. It gave a phone number he could call to get help. The brochure said that his call would be confidential.

Sergio called the number and subsequently attended a Criminals & Gangs Anonymous meeting in the back room of a nearby fire station. Two or three former gang members spoke. The stories they told sounded eerily similar to his own. During the discussion that followed, the group talked about why kids joined gangs and why gangs have such a powerful hold on people. Sergio didn't say a word. But his confidence in the program was growing. He reasoned that these people wouldn't be doing such dangerous work if they didn't care.

Sergio soon began to see the gang-rehab program as a real opportunity. Maybe it was his only chance to live to see his thirties. At the very least, it provided some small measure of hope. It showed Sergio that the barriers could be overcome. Tattoos could be removed. The church sponsoring the program would help cover the cost of tattoo removal and would provide medical support. King colors and symbols of gangsta power could be replaced with new clothing and jewelry. He could make new friends, situate himself in new surroundings, create a new identity, and discover a new way of looking at life.

Sergio got a job, again with the help of the people in the antigang organization. A network of former gang members encouraged him along the way.

Even more critical, he was beginning to learn some important things about himself. He saw the hateful condition of his own heart. He realized that he too was a sinner in need of forgiveness and healing. When he went to the weekly meetings, he heard about Jesus. The people who attended these meetings often read from the Bible. They quoted texts that held special meaning for them. The gospel's power was working a miracle in Sergio's own life.

Today Sergio is free from the terrible grip the Latin Kings once held on him. He has moved out of his old neighborhood, though he still maintains some contact with relatives. He may still be in danger in some quarters of Chicago. He reads his Bible and prays with other former gang members. As opportunities become available, Sergio speaks to young people still trapped in gangsta land. This cause is one for which he is willing to put his life at risk.

Some of the members of the antigang organization were once rivals of the Latin Kings—Sergio's sworn enemies. If they had walked onto Sergio's turf a year ago, he would have killed them on the spot. Today he sits next to them, works together with them, shares life with them, and prays with them. They are his brothers and sisters in Christ.

Speak to one another with psalms, hymns and spiritual songs. Sing and make music in your heart to the Lord, always giving thanks to God the Father for everything, in the name of our Lord Jesus Christ.

Ephesians 5:19,20

CHAPTER THREE

OF PEDESTALS AND OTHER HIGH PLACES

When I was in the sixth grade, I met Beethoven, Brahms, and Bach. We had an old RCA Victrola stored in the attic. I would disappear for hours so that I could spend time listening to the ancient 78-rpm recordings housed in the Victorian cabinet. Mozart, Tschaikovsky, and Mendelssohn were there, as were Chopin, Wagner, and Schubert.

This was the late fifties; 45-rpm singles were the rage. Rock 'n' roll was just starting to leave its mark on the American pop culture. My friends were listening to rock 'n' roll radio stations and dancing to the latest three-minute cuts from the Big Bopper, Elvis Presley, and Buddy Holly. I listened and learned to dance too. But when I wanted to indulge myself, I headed for the attic. There I would sit, fully absorbed in those scratchy, old, classical records.

My 78-rpm "friends" were able to transcend the centuries that lay between their times and mine. They spoke to me in a way that no one else ever had. Their songs were dynamic, profound, bold—yet gentle, alluring, honest, and passionate. In my heart I placed them on a pedestal, like the busts of famous people that adorned the drawing rooms of great mansions. I listened, mesmerized by their ideas; they talked to me in their music. They had no real solutions of their own, but they understood my life. They knew what it was to be human. They communicated with me in a way that soared high above the din of ordinary street life.

That same year the first wave of a great migration began. At first, just one or two black families moved in down the block. White homeowners panicked. Property values plummeted. Real estate agencies smelled opportunity, and the selling frenzy was on. Our neighborhood changed almost overnight. Eventually most of the houses on the block had either been sold or rented to African-American families.

A black couple—Hub and Mosse—rented the upper flat next door. They were good people—hard working, generous, kind to a fault. On Saturday mornings, Hub would light a heap of charcoal on his outdoor grill. Mosse would bring out a rack of spare ribs and let it slow cook over the coals all day. When the air was sweet with the bouquet of southern-style ribs, she would coax me over to the wire fence that separated our properties. Grinning, she would offer me a taste of the succulent meat. On those days my appreciation for African-American culture always increased.

The subject of race rarely came up at home. There wasn't much to discuss. My father's official position was that we were not supposed to see color in any people. That meant he saw no real difference between black folks and white folks. He was of the opinion that everyone deserved a chance to prove himself or herself, not on the basis of color but on the basis of decency and work ethic. But, in a less official way, we were encouraged to maintain a polite distance. This sentiment was often couched in the homespun expression "If you don't bother *them*, *they* won't bother you." Perhaps black parents said the same things to their children.

We were also schooled never to use the words *nigger, coon,* or *darky,* since African-Americans are offended by these words. Such words could hurt good people, we were told, even if we did not say them with that intent. But I took this concern to imply that the word *Negro* might also be offensive. We had to have several family talks to clarify which terminology was offensive and which was not. After that, I began referring to our new neighbors as *colored people* or *black people* —always in the most respectful way. I also quietly noted for myself that the differences between white people and black people seemed to have more to do with culture than skin color.

The big, gray house across the street was the first house on our block to be sold to a black family. The front porch was always full of toddlers, little kids, and teens, all laughing and having a good time. The family that lived there had moved to Milwaukee from Georgia or Alabama. I knew this because, to my ears, their Southern drawl was as unintelligible as French or Italian.

On Sundays the gray house became a gathering place for 50 to 60 people. They came early in the morning, dressed to the nines, and stayed late into the afternoon. The women brought platters of food. The men greeted one another warmly.

By midmorning the strains of Negro spirituals were pouring out the doors and windows and filling the streets with a rainbow of sound. The house itself appeared to sway from side to side in rhythm with the clapping and singing. When the music stopped, a preacher carried on for an hour or so. Then the music started in again, gathering momentum all afternoon. A female vocalist took turns with the congregation, *amen* and *hallelujah* punctuating each refrain.

White neighbors complained about the noise. A few just shook their heads, less irritated than confounded by the odd way these people expressed their faith. But I enjoyed it. Their music was so unlike anything I had ever experienced before. Their church may not have preached Bible truth in the same way as our Lutheran church, but their music pulsated with an energy and conviction that made me certain that they were filled with joy over the knowledge of their salvation in Christ.

Like breathing, our need to worship is compelling. We worship God with our decisions, our relationships, and our conduct. We worship formally or informally. We worship by hearing God's Word and receiving his sacraments. We worship with our prayers of supplication and our songs of thanksgiving. And then we repeat our worship all over again because of God's continued blessings and our unending desire to thank him.

The good news of salvation through Christ drives our worship. Jesus said his Father's altar could only be approached "in spirit and in truth" (John 4:24). The truth to which he was referring is that beautiful story of God's love for us—the gospel, and all the revealed truth of God's Word that the gospel embodies. In fact, the first axiom of worship is the knowledge that *God gives*. Our God is the God of our redemption—Christ, given *for us*. We are declared righteous on the basis of his accomplishments, not ours. And it is this truth that gives meaning to our lives and promises us life eternal in glory. With this truth God provides for all our spiritual needs. This truth comes to us in Baptism, bringing the gift of faith. This truth comes to us through God's Holy Word to comfort and encourage us. This truth comes to us in his body and blood, shed on the cross and given at the altar of his love. In fact, this truth is the inspiration for our worship. Could anyone who has been so deluged with blessings not be inclined to hold this God in the highest esteem? And, in the end, is there anything but worship that we are able to offer in humble response?

Our worship is what God wants. He desires our thankful, adoring hearts that give him the honor that only he deserves — nothing more, nothing less. The second axiom of Christian worship is this: *a grateful spirit offers the firstfruits of the heart.* That is what he deserves. No halfhearted efforts. No grudging afterthoughts. No second, third, or fourth place honors. No token gestures. No halvsies or leftovers. No reserved sentiments. Excellence — the best we have to offer — not measured by man's standards but by God's holy and just standard.

Of course, even our best efforts fail to measure up. God is looking for an excellence to match his excellency. Perfect and holy, he will receive only that which is also perfect and holy. In truth, the only human act of worship that has ever met God's standard was found in Jesus. His righteous life and sacrificial death were the ultimate in human worship. He gave all honor and glory to the Father where we could not. When the Spirit of Jesus took up residence in the temple of our bodies, he sanitized our hearts with the blood of Jesus and offered his perfect worship in our names. With the power of his forgiveness, we are able to recognize that God deserves the place above anything else that threatens to take precedence in our lives. We gladly give him our best efforts. Cleansed in his blood, our own worship, feeble and tainted though it may be, is accepted as perfect and holy in God's sight.

In ancient times a farmer's firstfruits might have included a quantity of grain taken early in the harvest (Proverbs 3:9). (His act of worship then was actually also an act of trust. A sudden hailstorm could wipe out the rest of his crop, leaving his family to starve.) But, for the sake of discussion, let's imagine that you work in the field of, say . . . language. Perhaps you hire out as a wordsmith—a poet, fashioning ideas into phrases and sentences that communicate your ideas to other people. What would be the firstfruits of your grateful heart?

That's easy. You would dedicate your finest ideas to God.

God's people have been expressing their love for God in just that way for thousands of years. They have been offering him the best of their ideas, from Solomon's grand temple to the gothic cathedrals of Europe, from Greek orthodox icons to the stained-glass windows in many Lutheran churches, from King David's psalms to Handel's *The Messiah*.

In this way, over the centuries, the church has sown and harvested a worship culture of its own—a firstfruits of the ages, as it were. This culture consists of a whole corpus of ideas: rituals, music, poetry, service orders, art, architecture. And it derives from a diverse cross section of Christian persuasions, including Roman Catholic, Lutheran, Arminian, and Reformed. Thus, the invisible church of God—past, present and future—is united together with one voice, expressing its thanks and praise in a rich accumulation of forms from across the ages. For two thousand years, the worship of the Christian church has transformed the common stuff of contemporary life to a level of excellence that transcends the ordinary. As one might imagine, having been drawn from 20 centuries of Christianity and a broad range of sources, these offerings are also culturally and historically diverse. And their diversity raises an interesting question.

Worship emanates from a deep personal relationship between the individual and his God. Yet, because we are social creatures, we can share the joys of faith with one another in a group setting. In a perfect world, we would agree on our worship choices. But among sinner-saints, whenever two or more Christians come together to worship, they will first need to ask, *"How* will *we* worship *together?"* And this is not the kind of question that should be determined by rank or status, where one Christian lords it over another. Answering this question requires a shared desire to offer God our best ideas.

In Old Testament times, with the best interest of his people at heart, God provided a solution to that question. He prescribed a format that addressed the *how*, *where*, and *when* of Hebrew worship. Old Testament believers needed plenty of symbols (the scapegoat, the Pascal Lamb, bloody sacrifices, incense, the Most Holy Place in the temple) pointing them to the coming Messiah. The Lord embedded foreshadows of Christ in the tabernacle, poetry, festivals, and rituals of everyday Jewish life.

In the New Testament era, however, we are free to make our own worship decisions. God gives us this freedom for our own good, even as his prescribed worship for Old Testament believers was intended for their good. Our New Testament freedom introduces a third element of worship. The apostle Paul said it plainly: "Speak to one another with psalms, hymns and spiritual songs. Sing and make music in your heart to the Lord, always giving thanks to God the Father for everything, in the name of our Lord Jesus Christ" (Ephesians 5:19,20).

Paul is clearly talking about worship. His first word *(speak)* already tips us off to his overarching theme, which is communication. Most of Paul's words are an eloquent echo of the first and second elements of worship. He points to the gospel as the driving force in our worship. We are to be "always giving thanks," he said, for everything the Father gives us in Jesus' name. (We'll get back to "Jesus' name" in a minute.)

Look carefully. The words *one another* add yet another focus. Paul is talking about our communication with one another, not our communication with God. God already knows what lies within our hearts. He knows our thoughts, even before they pass through our minds, but others do not. In congregational worship, what we say to one another is important. We need to know what others are thinking and feeling. We need to hear their confessions of faith, and they need to hear ours. We need to be instructed in the revealed truth that brought us together. So, *in group worship, we proclaim God's revealed truth to one another.* This is the third axiom of worship.

Sounds easy. But, in today's world, often described as a global community, good communication is anything but easy.

Music,[2] both secular and sacred, has stood for centuries as a powerful language. Music says a lot about us as individuals and as God's people. And it does so in profoundly powerful ways.

Music is a vehicle for self-expression within a social setting. People identify with their ethnic and national cultures through music (Bohemian polka, Irish jig, Brazilian tango). During the last century, many emerging subcultures also sprang up and were identified with specific musical styles (country/western, blues, Dixieland, bluegrass, folk, alternative, punk rock, heavy metal, rap). As cultures divide and subdivide like living cells, the explosion of cultural diversity has created a lush smorgasbord from which to pick and choose. In the secular realm, there is so much diversity that all varieties of music enjoy almost equal standing. Even so-called *highbrow* has been relegated to just another choice.

Most of us sidled up to our favorite musical genres fairly early in life. We may have even constructed our public identity, at least in part, around the musical ideas we claimed as "my kind of music." (Many products of the fifties chose to identify themselves with recording artists like Elvis Presley or Roy Orbison. I still identify with classical music. But, probably due to my childhood experiences in the central city, I am also very fond of the blues.)

We should not be too surprised to find this "my kind of music" mentality creeping into the church. For some, that means a traditional musical menu — hymns, chorales, psalm settings. For others, my kind of music means something more like folk songs, spirituals, children's songs, and the like. When care is given to elevate a genre above the ordinary street connections, God-pleasing worship might conceivably include music with a heavy backbeat or something as contemporary as rap. In any case, the "my kind of music" mentality is becoming a divisive issue. Many church bodies struggle to find musical genres that will give all members opportunity to proclaim the gospel—each in his or her own way—without alienating members steeped in denominational tradition.

Some fear that, in an effort to suit everybody's needs, we may forget the value of the wonderful accumulation of excellent compositions produced over the centuries. They argue that our musical heritage not only transcends languages and cultures but also time. They are correct in pointing out that, when we come together in Jesus' name, we truly are in communion with all believers of all times—past, present, and future. To lose touch with our past is to dismember Christ's body. They are also correct in noting that much musical material not from that tradition has a history clouded with doctrinal error or pagan unbelief.

Hymns and chorales are the main body of our cherished Lutheran musical heritage. They are genuine treasures—the trappings of a distinct religious culture. They proclaim the message of Lutheranism by teaching its doctrines in musical texts. We can, and should, be thankful for them. We should work tirelessly in an effort never to lose them. These truly are gifts from God that contribute to an overall sense of belonging, providing us with part of our identity. They speak clearly and intensely to the world in which we live.

But today's world celebrates diversity. As we make our musical choices for worship, should we view that diversity as a threat or a blessing? As we search for new ways of speaking to one another in psalms, hymns, and spiritual songs, we will be forced to examine a wider range of music drawn from the ordinary "stuff" of life. The best of these new resources can be transformed into the firstfruits of all of God's people, even though that stuff may not always flow out of the Lutheran tradition.

However, those who are especially sensitive to the needs of people new to the faith are also correct. They point out that those of us who have a more mature faith need to temper our worship decisions with concern for the needs of the weak, the young, and the fragile in faith. This too is an act of selfless love (see chapter 4). When a similar issue arose in the early church, the apostle James spoke up, saying, "We should not make it difficult for the Gentiles who are turning to God" (Acts 15:19).

To some, a culturally diverse approach sounds more like a prescription for disunity than unity. On any given Sunday, a service might include a choir anthem from the 17th century, a popular children's song, a 19th-century hymn rendered in the classical Lutheran tradition, and a teen choir singing a psalm setting accompanied by guitar and drums. All this within a well-planned worship framework.

And so, the tension builds. Those with one perspective argue that the introduction of popular musical genres into Lutheran worship either emotionalizes worship or emphasizes praise over proclamation. The other side argues that too much analysis of the historical background of a song intellectualizes worship. An undercurrent of voices keeps the pressure on a congregation's decision makers with the reminder that New Testament believers have a blood-bought freedom to decide how they will worship.

A third factor makes finding a point of balance in this discussion even more complex. People today are extremely interested in exploring their historic origins. This isn't just a phenomenon within the Christian church. In recent years, for example, there has been a notable interest in ancient Celtic drones, not to mention ancient myths and literature. People want to celebrate their ancestral beginnings. This trend also has an impact on our worship decisions.

One solution is to make sure that we continually elevate some of the new stuff from our contemporary culture to a level of excellence that transcends the ordinary. The best of these new contributions can then be integrated into a church's musical cornucopia.

There is another solution—one that drives us back to our concern for one another. Our love for one another seeks to provide resolution wherever there is tension. We cannot really speak the truth to one another without the selfless gospel love of Jesus in our hearts. That is what Paul meant when he added the phrase "in the name of our Lord Jesus Christ" (Ephesians 5:20). Expressions like "*my* kind of music" have no currency among new creatures in Christ, not if those words betray a lack of concern that *my* kind of music may exclude others from the joys of corporate worship.

A few years ago the members of our church's teen group were invited to participate in a contemporary worship service on Mother's Day. The service didn't follow traditional service orders, but the planning and preparation demonstrated an earnest desire to maintain a gospel focus. The musical portions of the service made use of a guitar and snare drums to provide an up-tempo accompaniment. The service went smoothly. The content was consistent throughout—never shallow, always grounded in God's Word. The emphasis was clearly *God for us*. In terms of planning and preparation, the excellence was obvious. The message was powerful, and the service was generally accepted by most of the members. A handful, however, were troubled by the contemporary music style. At least one member was overheard to say, "Drums have no place in our church's worship services."

We may have our personal preferences—our cultural comfort zones—but the worship choices we make for congregational life need to be made for the good of all. In love, a Christian congregation can embrace a full range of materials that will give all its members an opportunity to proclaim the gospel, each in his or her own unique way. For those who will have difficulty making this adjustment, Saint Paul offers these words of encouragement: "I can do everything through him who gives me strength" (Philippians 4:13). In Christ, we can even learn to be more open minded about the various musical styles we employ in worshiping our Lord.

Finally, the tension here is, in some ways, healthy. As we harvest the best ideas from a culture rich in raw materials, God is also teaching us to appreciate the diversity of gifts that he has distributed among us. By filling our hearts with love for one another, he provides a way for us to work together toward resolving our worship choices. God gives. In this case he also gives us the ability to rise above our personal biases to worship him together in diverse ways with one voice.

Jonathan Swift once wrote, "Vision is the art of seeing things invisible." From her earliest childhood days, Mary had vision. She imagined things invisible—majestic sounds, in particular. And those sounds brought new meaning and truth to her young life. It might even be said that Mary had a *vision*— one which recurred throughout her young life. And in her youth, that vision slowly grew to become her art.

When Mary was growing up, Watseka, Illinois, was little more than a village. Situated a hundred miles south of Chicago, it lies smack in the middle of America's heartland. There was sandlot baseball to occupy a kid's time, but not much else. Mary's family didn't own a television. They didn't get a record player until the late fifties. And for a year or more after they finally did purchase that phonograph, the family record collection consisted of only one album: Tschaikovsky's *Sleeping Beauty*.

For recreation, Mary's family sang. They loved to sing church music—chorales and cantatas—the music of Bach and Mendelssohn. Mary never thought of her family as eccentric or their musical diversion as out of the ordinary. To her it was all just part of growing up.

Mary's older brother attended school at Concordia College in Milwaukee. He sang in the male chorus. Frequently the touring choir presented a festival concert in a town near Mary's. Her family attended those concerts whenever they could. Some of the more influential names in Lutheran musical tradition became as familiar to Mary as the names of baseball greats like Ted Williams, Ernie Banks, and Joe DiMaggio. After one of the concerts, Mary's parents invested in a recording of the Concordia College Choir singing Handel's *The Messiah*. They also acquired a vocal score of Handel's great musical work and routinely incorporated it into their family sing-alongs. They worked on their respective parts and were able to produce a pleasant, if not thoroughly refined, sound.

Though her mother persisted in making Mary practice the piano, this was far from Mary's first love in life. Even her love for baseball came in second to the real desire of Mary's young heart, which was to conduct her own choir in a rendition of *The Messiah.*

Through the years she had accumulated a motley collection of candle figurines — Thanksgiving turkeys, Santa Clauses, reindeer, pumpkins, angels, evergreen trees. These were the members of Mary's imaginary chorus. With the recording of *The Messiah* playing in the background, Mary directed the complete score from memory. Each figurine was assigned its proper place among the sopranos, altos, tenors, or basses. They were carefully aligned on risers made of cardboard boxes. Rehearsals were carefully orchestrated down to the correct marching order for her wax processionals. Nothing was left to chance. And, although the choir's performances were rarely given for more than one or two family members, George Frideric Handel himself would have been proud. They were terrific! In her own imagination, Mary had created a way to bring Handel's music to life through her little wax choir. Her performance flowed from a child's uncomplicated and unsophisticated faith. Her simple wax offering was truly a firstfruit of her grateful heart.

Submit to one another
out of reverence for Christ.

Ephesians 5:21

CHAPTER FOUR

Humble Pie

The gap between 10-year-olds and 13-year-olds is huge. There's no defense against a kid who is three or four years older than you and twice your size, no matter how many of you there are. My brother Ren, our friend Joey, and I had managed to dodge Dirk for a week. We may have outnumbered him, but that didn't matter. Even together we lacked the courage to stand up to him. What was worse, Dirk knew we were afraid of him. And we knew he knew. We had done nothing to provoke him. We were just younger and smaller. If the word on the streets was accurate, sooner or later he would get around to us.

Bullies were not uncommon on Brown Street turf. There, every boy eventually toughened. But our toughness hadn't matured yet, so troublemakers practiced on us.

Eventually the three of us wound up lying facedown on the asphalt in a remote part of the playground. It was my first taste of oppression. It left a bitter aftertaste. The whole idea of being subjected to someone else's will made me sick to my stomach. For more than an hour, Dirk kept us squirming under his control. There wasn't much point to it. He didn't demand money or try to force us to participate in some unspeakable sex act. This was a manifestation of sheer meanness. Every few minutes he would push his sneaker down against the nape of my neck, grinding my face into the hot pavement again.

We were humiliated . . . so humiliated that we vowed never to breathe a word of it to anyone. (It occurs to me that I am actually breaking that vow as I write.)

But something else happened that same day which is also tattooed permanently on my memory. Marty was the smallest and youngest member of our little gang, sometimes *in*, sometimes on the fringe—a wannabe. The bullies generally ignored Marty. There was no prestige in picking on a fat, little Jewish boy. But Marty was the perfect target for healing my damaged pride. My ego needed reinflating, so I went looking for him.

When I found Marty, I treated him the same way Dirk had treated the three of us. My approach was more subtle, but nonetheless, it was still oppression. I threatened him. I told Marty I would turn everyone in our club against him, maybe even get him thrown out. I worked on his insecurity. I used his desperate need to belong as leverage. I wanted him to squirm. I wanted it to be clear to him that I was in control.

In retrospect, the most important lesson of the day was that my own heart could be as black as any thug's.

Human relationships often involve domination—not that that is always wrong. Some relationships are meant to be that

42

way—for example, relationships among the ranks of the military, between teachers and students, and between parents and children. Paul also describes that kind of relationship between Christ and his people (Ephesians 5:23,24). Often these are relationships in which the authority someone exercises over another is God ordained. But every relationship in which one person has dominion over another also has the potential for tyranny.

All people quite naturally recognize tyranny as a common enemy. Some of us tyrannize others by manipulation. We threaten, posture, bribe, or conspire until we get our way. Some of us may even resort to brute force. This desire to control another person's will seems to proceed from a dark corner of our psyches. We instinctively recognize only two positions in our relationships—*dominator* and *dominated*. Even Christians find it difficult to see their relationships in any other way. We chafe at the thought of submitting to the will of another—especially to the will of a bully. Facedown on the asphalt is just not the place to be. We learn that already in childhood.

Many parents consider this an important lesson for their children to learn. Many fathers and mothers want their children to be assertive and, in some settings, even aggressive. For a few, training their children to "kick ass" ranks high on their list of parenting priorities. They vow, "No child of mine is going to spend life on the bottom of the heap."

Power and influence often make the difference between being secure and being miserable. In our little club, we learned quickly that official membership was subject to the whims of whoever happened to be in power at the time. It was politics, pure and simple. The key was to become part of the decision-making process. In that way one could control those weighty decisions rather than be controlled. That was my advantage over Marty; I operated near the top of the decision-making pyramid. He didn't.

This dynamic offered a fairly accurate projection of the adult world that awaited us. The gears of life in the military, the corporate world, or organized crime are all greased with the same set of rules. Each of us is trapped in some kind of hierarchy. It's how things work: powerful or subservient, dominator or dominated.

This is also an honest description of how God's church on earth works. It would be inaccurate and misleading to suggest that God's kingdom on earth operates in some other mystical fashion. The word *hierarchy* does apply in some ways. In fact, it is a prerequisite to good order. A church's polity functions according to a decision-making structure that is based on real, biblical authority.

And, yes, the Lord Jesus is in command. But he also delegates. In most congregations a constitution determines how a core of individuals (called, elected, or appointed) governs the day-to-day ministry to God's people. Christians need to understand how they fit in and function within that framework.

A simple biblical principle influences our posture toward one another within that people-of-God structure called the church. Let's consider that principle now.

Even for Christians the word *submit* goes down hard, like a fishbone caught sideways in the throat. Every fiber in our being resists the thought of submitting. We desire autonomy. We want control over our own destinies. Submission puts us under someone else's control. Yet, difficult as it may be to swallow, submission is at the very heart of every godly relationship.

Understand, this is not the same as the forced submission I exacted from Marty. Christlike subordination is completely voluntary. It is submissive nonetheless, but borne entirely out of love. Only those who have been transformed into new creatures by Christ's forgiving love can assume this unlikely attitude.

Our Lord Jesus was the picture of such humble submission. Even when his suffering and death were only hours away, Jesus possessed all his heavenly power (John 13:3). Imagine having heaven's complete arsenal of divine weaponry at your disposal! Jesus was not only fully armed; he also had the authority to use his weapons. No human has ever had that potential for wielding real power. Not Moses. Not David. Not Solomon. Not Samson or Elijah. Not the apostles or Mary. But Jesus had it, and he knew it. Nothing could have stopped him had he taken a notion to blow the whole world to hell. How tempting that must have been! By human standards he had plenty of reasons to do just that. He was about to die for the crimes of others—an injustice of the most unforgivable kind. The holy Son of God was about to be ridiculed, beaten, scorned, scoffed at, stripped naked, and executed as a common criminal—all on behalf of his sworn enemies!

Now, as the darkness was rapidly enveloping him, we are told that he had the power to change the direction of those horrible events. He could have ended it before it all exploded in his face. He has the power do anything he wants. He could have proven, once and for all, that he is in control of all things. As the almighty King, he could have reclaimed his dominion over all things.

What did Jesus do? Certainly not what any of us would have done, given such a commanding position. He got up quietly and washed the feet of his own students, including the feet of Judas, who had hatred in his heart and betrayal on his mind. Slaves normally carried out this humble task. A king would never consider washing the feet of his subjects. It was a sign of weakness—a gesture of humility and total subjugation. But that is what our King did. In the end, he forfeited life itself, voluntarily submitting to the will of his heavenly Father.

Now, look at Jesus. He leads by example. He is our model for humble submission. Ponder his posture at the feet of his followers—on his knees before them, head bowed, hands eager to serve. Join him there. Put yourself at someone else's disposal. Submit. Study what it means to put the needs of another before your own. Step aside and let the other guy get ahead of you in line. Play second fiddle . . . or third . . . or fourth. Look at your relationships in this new light. Think of yourself as the one dominating others; then think of yourself as the one who is being dominated. Saint Paul wrote:

> Each of you should look not only to your own interests, but also to the interests of others.

> Your attitude should be the same as that of Christ Jesus: Who, being in very nature God, did not consider equality with God something to be grasped, but made himself nothing, taking the very nature of a servant, being made in human likeness. And being found in appearance as a man, he humbled himself and became obedient to death—even death on a cross! (Philippians 2:4-8)

Clothe yourself with that attitude of submission day in and day out. It's a godly perspective. When you do, your relationships with others will immediately begin to change.

Submitting to others is a foundational concept in Christ's church on earth. While voluntary submission turns secular thinking on its ear, one can rightly expect such an attitude among God's people. Yet even new creatures in Christ are not always the models of humble submission that God would have us be. Occasionally there are bullies among us. Some of them are even well-intentioned bullies. Others, driven by their own self-interests, clearly lead by intimidation. I have seen them, bold and strutting, among the clergy and among those in positions of leadership. I have also observed them, cunning and sly, cowardly operating behind closed doors. They come on the attack, Bible in hand, seeking power and influence, undermining genuine authority, confusing members, acting like Absalom at the gate (2 Samuel 15). For some, it is a personality quirk. For others, it is a curse that comes with the lust for honor and authority. By God's grace, such aberrations are relatively rare. But when power mongers are permitted to have their way among God's people, the effect on real ministry can be devastating.

Others among us have difficulty knowing when to lead and when to be good followers. We speak when we should listen and fail to speak when the moment to lead presents itself. Either way, we enable tyranny to have its way.

What I have described is a problem of the heart. It is a problem with which every individual Christian needs to wrestle. To our own shame, many of us deserve to be numbered among the bullies at one time or another. But we also may need to come clean regarding our sins of omission, for there are also those times when we should have taken a stand and failed to do so.

Jesus shed his blood to remove the stains of these sins. With the power of his forgiveness, he can give us the courage to stand boldly, even alone in a room full of opposition if need be, and to speak the truth.

In a sinful world, the threat of a tyrant rising up and raising Cain in God's house is very real. Tyrants can appear innocent and sound learned and wise. They almost always appear to be powerful. Their methods are the way of the cult leader.

God's people cannot afford to be deceived. Demagoguery sows the seeds of rancor and division. When it occurs, kingdom work is compromised in a thousand ways.

Tyranny thrives on insecurity. It feeds on weakness. The antidote is hidden in the power of God's Word. When God's people study Scripture and have a firm foundation in God's truth, bullies cannot get a foothold.

Sooner or later, we are all cast in a leadership role, even if that is only within the family context. The line between good Christian leadership and tyranny is sometimes precariously thin. The idea here is not to see how close we can come to the line. The idea is to remain as far from becoming tyrants as we possibly can—to lead with conviction and confidence but remain humble toward those whom we serve.

Tyranny is unacceptable in God's family. Paul is speaking to all of us when he urges, "Submit to one another out of reverence for Christ" (Ephesians 5:21). Humility is one of the character traits Jesus looks for when he hires workers for his vineyard. "For he who is least among you all—he is the greatest" (Luke 9:48). Jesus sees us doing our best work at the bottom of the pile. That is where he did his best work.

I pitied Lars from the very first day I met him. And I had a hard time understanding why others had so much respect for him. The poor man had no backbone. Day in and day out

Estelle would badger him and make demands that went far beyond the limit of a supportive husband's role. "Lars, I have a hair appointment in a half hour. Don't forget." "Lars, stop what you're doing this instant and make lunch for me."

Now Lars was a busy man. He had many responsibilities. The folks in town thought highly of his calm approach to finance and his levelheaded way of resolving business disputes. He was a friend, a mentor, and a confidante.

Lars was also an elder statesman in the church. He taught Sunday school, served on several boards and committees, and ushered on Sunday mornings. He always had a smile on his face and a cheerful greeting for all. But Lars had this singular character flaw, and it was not a discrete matter. In fact, it had become a regular feature of the daily gossip in town. People would watch and wait for the next outrageous demand Estelle would serve up for old Lars. Her expectations were often so ridiculous that they were hard to believe. Just when you had heard a story that seemed to stretch reason to the limit, someone would come along and corroborate the story, giving new life to the unseemly legend. It was funny in a way. But, in another way, we all felt a real sense of compassion for old Lars. He was in an impossible situation — of his own making, of course.

Some of us felt compelled to be miserable, as surrogates of a sort, on Lars' behalf. A few of us even considered correcting Estelle ourselves, but we quickly dismissed the thought. None of us had that kind of courage! So we went on hoping against hope that Lars would just once take a stand, that he would dig in and set the record straight with Estelle.

And, once or twice he almost did. Then, at the last moment, he would back down and lose another chunk of face in his retreat.

Christian wedding vows put the husband at the head of a Christian household. In the case of Lars and Estelle, that model seemed to have been thrown in reverse. Had Lars chosen to look for some peace of mind by leaving Estelle, he would have had plenty of sympathizers, even from within the church. But Lars seemed to see his marriage in a different light. His willingness to cater to Estelle's every whim reflected another kind of biblical wisdom. In love, he recognized that Estelle would never be able to change. "That's just Estelle," he would say. It was a permanent part of the package that he had agreed to long ago when he said *I do*. He had resigned himself to that fact from the very beginning. Perhaps he even found something akin to joy in subjugating himself to her unreasonable whims. Slowly I found myself beginning to admire him for that.

When Lars died I couldn't help but feel a sense of relief on his behalf. He was finally free from Estelle's ridiculous demands. But I also felt a real sense of loss. Lars had been a model of patience and humility for us all. He had shown us how love can drive a person far beyond the limits of what is reasonable. He had taught us how to submit, even when it was not required by the letter of the law. He had shown us just how far one might go in maintaining a subordinate position in a relationship—the position in which Jesus sees us doing our best work.

Honor one another above yourselves.

Romans 12:10

CHAPTER FIVE

THE WHEELSTICK

When I was seven years old, my grandfather made a toy for me. He called it a *wheelstick*. Wheelstick seemed to be just the right name because that was essentially what this contraption was — an old discarded wheelbarrow wheel to which he had attached a 3-foot length of 1- by 2-inch lumber, using a stove bolt.

My grandfather was all about exquisite workmanship. Carefully cutting the stick, precisely drilling the hole, and painstakingly searching for cotter pins and washers that fit just right consumed an entire Saturday morning. I know this because I watched him make it. When he was done, a proud grin spread across his mustached face. He handed my new wheelstick to me with the pomp and ceremony generally reserved for extravagant gifts.

We dragged the thing up the basement stairs and took it outside where he showed me how a wheelstick worked. Basically, you just pushed it down the sidewalk. That was all there was to it. For my brother Ren, he made another one—a slightly smaller version with a smaller wheel and a shorter stick. Presumably this was because Ren was younger and, therefore, unable to handle the larger deluxe model.

My brother and I looked at each other with dismay. This device may have served a fine purpose a quarter of a century earlier, during the Great Depression, when my dad and his brothers were growing up. It might even have been the rage of the neighborhood back then, but this was the fifties. All my friends had bicycles or wagons—wheeled vehicles that could actually transport people or things from here to there. What good was a wheelstick? It couldn't transport a thing.

I played with my wheelstick for about ten seconds and then unceremoniously abandoned it. I did this with a lot of disdain too, not for my grandfather but for his invention. Though I cannot remember what I said, I'm sure I hurt his feelings. So did Ren. We had absolutely no use for wheelsticks or any other outmoded ideas Grandpa wanted to foist on us. We were embarrassed to be seen in public with these things. Kids might discover us bookin' down the sidewalk with our wheelsticks and laugh. So we buried them in a heap of junk in the back of the old tin garage.

I still feel a little pinch of guilt over my haughty attitude toward that wheelstick. I should have been more sensitive. I might have shown some interest. It wouldn't have hurt to experiment with the thing for a while longer, just to find out if it had any redeeming value.

Asian people have a sharper conscience about things like honor. They would say I had dishonored my grandfather. And perhaps they would be right. I can still see the look of disappointment on my grandfather's face.

There were a lot of other occasions when I honored his memory. I think of him today with the utmost affection and respect. He was a beacon of faith. I could see that even as a seven-year-old. He was a gentleman, a solid citizen, a lover of life. But on that infamous day, when I received the wheelstick, I dishonored his memory.

My grandfather's life was a rich collection of personal experiences. He worked in a foundry as a tool and die maker and survived two world wars. He helped build a new church, making the lighting fixtures and ironwork gratings in his own basement. He loved his Savior and his family. He enjoyed people and was always singing or laughing. That is how I remember him. He died when I was eight. In the short time we had together, he left a deep impression on me. A half century later, I still honor his memory.

It takes character to suspend concentration on one's own story long enough to learn about someone else's. It requires energy and self-discipline to put one's own relative importance on hold. Yet, when we do, real communication begins to take place.

Today deep listening is becoming a lost art. We have neither the time nor the interest. Expressions of care and compassion are disappearing with it. Maybe forever. We are just so consumed with self-interest. Many of us barely function at the level of polite, sociable conversation. We are simply bored with the things others have to say. The only story that really matters to most of us is our own. Of course, no one is listening to our story either. So we each go on believing that we have almost nothing in common with one another. Is it any wonder that we have such a difficult time sharing our emotions or the deepest convictions of our souls? What a pity! How much we are missing! There are so many moving stories to be heard—all of them relevant to our understanding of one another's struggles in life.

The Fourth Commandment is the first of the commandments to discuss human relationships. It begins with the words *Honor your father and mother.* Honor apparently has a connection with family. By inference we might even suggest that honor can be linked to the passing of values from one generation to the next. We might even conclude that the Fourth Commandment makes it incumbent on each generation to listen to what those who have already lived have to say about life. We are likely to encounter many of the same obstacles and challenges that our ancestors have already faced. God expects us to consider their wisdom. That is one way we honor them.

Our generation has forgotten to do that. In that sense, we have collectively dishonored our ancestors.

Too many of us apply the Fourth Commandment only to our children. We recognize its value as a stern reminder for our children to behave as we want them to behave. We use it to reinforce our authority over them. That is, of course, also an application of the Fourth Commandment.

But the principle of honoring applies to adults in ways that go profoundly beyond the force of authority. We adults need to relearn what it means to *honor* our fathers and our mothers, our grandpas and grandmas, our ancestors. And we especially need to relearn what it means to honor the memory of those who nurtured faith within us—our spiritual ancestors, if you will. Such honoring occurs when we pass the gospel, and all the values that flow from it, to the next generation. We might call it *generational evangelism*.

Listening is the prelude to telling. Compassionate listening is a component of effective communication. Granted, planting faith is always a miracle of God's Holy Spirit. But understanding the people with whom we share the healing message of the gospel is essential. We need to learn where others hurt and why. We need to hear their stories to have a sense of what their life experiences have already taught them. We need to learn their languages and study their cultures and their subcultures. We do not have to adopt their ways. But we do need to make a sincere effort to understand what they are all about so we can speak in a way that they can understand. That only happens when we take the time to listen to them and learn more about them. If that means spending long hours with them to gain insights into their issues and struggles, we need to do that. To simply charge in and begin preaching Christ, without getting to know the people to whom we are speaking, may very well appear rude and arrogant. It sends the wrong signals, and it flies in the face of godly compassion.

Saint Paul urges us to honor one another *above ourselves*. He means that we ought to work harder to ensure that others receive the honor due them than we work for our own honor. To accomplish that, we need to invest time and energy in others. We must suspend our own self-interests long enough to really get to know one another in an effort to share Jesus.

The kids who spend time at Calvary Academy in South Milwaukee are hardened in rebellion. When I met Kip, he was still a ward of the county. He had been at the academy for almost eight months. Since he had an eight-year history of running away from foster homes and correctional facilities, I wondered at the risk. Would an off-campus trip to a nearby restaurant give him another chance to run? The academy, however, had been most cooperative in setting up this interview. Now the pressure was on me to dig deep enough to find a story worth sharing with others.

I tried to relax as the soft-spoken young man pointed the way to a mom-and-pop place two miles up the road. Conversation was easy, even though both of us were nervous.

I asked for a booth so there would be plenty of opportunity to make eye contact. He was a good-looking kid — put together well. His round, boyish face featured an inviting smile. He talked slowly and deliberately. I liked him right away.

I don't like to spend a lot of time making small talk during interviews. I figured we both understood the purpose of this lunch meeting. Still, there is no easy way to ask a complete stranger to tell you his life story. As the waitress poured our first cups of coffee, I explained what I had in mind. I was writing this book . . . pseudonyms could be used . . . just looking for some true stories. I prefer to let my subject ramble. One or two well-phrased questions is usually all I need. I started in abruptly, hoping this question would generate momentum. "What was your home life like when you were little?"

The food came, awkwardly interrupting the pregnant moment. The question hung, suspended in midconversation, dangling out there like bait. I invited Kip to pray out loud with me. We began together: "Come, Lord Jesus . . ." He knew the words, and he wasn't shy about saying them with me. I realized I was testing him. Calvary Academy is owned and operated by an association of Lutheran churches. I assumed table prayers were part of their daily routine. I wanted to see how this young man would react to an invitation to pray with a fellow Christian outside the academy's circle of control. He passed the test. I felt ashamed for using prayer in such a manipulative way.

Kip needed only my opening prompt. He was eager to share his life, even if it was with a total stranger. As he spoke, I mentally cataloged the details of his story. Although his words were unrehearsed, the 17-year-old seemed to anticipate everything I expected.

Kip's mother and father had divorced when he was eight. His father had a problem with alcohol and a propensity for physical abuse. The words *physical abuse* caught in Kip's throat as he said them. He swallowed hard, his dark eyes wincing.

Kip had been the family "goat," taking the blame for just about everything that went wrong at home. He had been beaten and verbally humiliated too many times to count. But because Kip took the brunt of his father's anger, his brother (18 months younger) remained largely unscathed. "It's amazing that my brother and I can be so different and still be as close as we are," he noted.

Shortly after his parent's divorce, Kip began to have trouble at school. His grades dropped. He was involved in fights almost daily, both on the playground and in the classroom. He threatened his teachers. To avoid the disciplinary hassles at school, Kip began inventing excuses to stay home. Being truant only made it harder for him to keep up with his classes. The frustrations of academic failure intensified Kip's anger.

Many things were breaking down for Kip at the same time—family relationships, support from school, social interaction. And Kip's raging anger always seemed to be at the center of the breakdown. It was a theme that would repeat itself over and over throughout the interview.

Kip's story is similar to those of thousands of other kids across the country! As he talked, I wondered what, if anything, made his story unique. Kip's only way to express himself was through violent behavior. His anger consumed him and controlled him. Occasionally the rage was self-directed, but most of the time Kip's anger exploded randomly—especially when someone dared to hold him accountable for his actions.

Kip was living with his mother at the time his fighting landed him in juvenile court. She admitted to the court that she couldn't control him. Kip was sent to live with his father, but the two fought constantly. Eventually Kip ran away.

Soon Kip found himself living in foster homes and correctional institutions, spending shorter periods of time either with his mother, who was now engaged to a man Kip did not like, or with his abusive father. The narration of each episode ended with the same sad phrase, droned like a mantra: "That didn't go well either."

By his 11th birthday, Kip had become friends with members of the Gangsta Disciples (GDs). He spent time hanging out with them and getting high—sometimes three, four, or five nights a week. His friends sponsored his initiation as a Disciple. Kip used the expression *being brought-in*. Being brought-in involved picking up eight pennies from the ground while GDs punched and kicked him in the head, face, and midsection. It was a hard way to find acceptance, but getting brought-in meant that Kip finally had a family.

By the time Kip was 14, he had seen the inside of several correctional facilities. Some had helped him. A stay for several months in Wyalusing State Correctional Facility helped relieve his adolescent depression. Other facilities, though, only hardened him more. Back on the street, he would return to his GD friends and their lifestyle, which quickly led to marijuana and alcohol use. Yet Kip remained determined not to become involved with hard drugs.

During his 15th year, Kip was shuttled from one foster home to another. In one of these homes, he loaned money for drugs to some of his foster brothers. When they refused to pay him back, he took out two of them in an outburst of violence. One ended up with a broken nose; the other, with a gash that required stitches. Somehow Kip beat the battery charge in court.

His father had always been the focus for Kip's anger. But when his father received treatment for depression and alcoholism, Kip agreed to try living with him again. Things went well for a while, but Kip's father was still a suspicious man, quick to jump to conclusions. When Kip went camping with some of his friends, his father stormed into the campsite, accusing Kip of drinking and partying hard. The accusation was not true. Kip went to his father's house, grabbed his things, and never looked back.

Kip then lived with his grandmother for a while until he got picked up for driving without a license. His probation officer had run out of patience. This time Kip faced time in a much more serious place.

Kip described his parents as nominal Christians: they belonged to a Lutheran church in town but never attended. However, his grandmother was a religious person. When she learned about Calvary Academy, she encouraged Kip to suggest it to his probation officer as an option. His probation officer agreed but added several qualifying clauses to the contract. For one, Kip could not run away again.

The interview was going so well I didn't want to slow things down. Had I let him, the young man would have talked nonstop without taking a single bite of his food. I told him to take a break so that he could eat some of the gyro sandwich he had ordered.

It quickly became clear that Kip was a bright kid. He was very articulate in sharing his story with me—careful to keep things in order. He told me he was maintaining a 3.5-plus GPA at the academy. I had no reason to doubt him. He said he didn't want to settle for a GED as some kids were inclined to do. His goal was to graduate from high school and go on to college. He was thinking about majoring in business.

I asked Kip if any of this was painful to talk about. "The stuff with my mother and my father is," he said. The cold, matter-of-fact way in which he said it made me believe it was even hard for him to say the words *mother* and *father*. "I know I've messed up, so I can talk about that. But there's some stuff I can't talk about because it still hurts too much. And there's other stuff I won't talk about because I don't want to get my friends in trouble. I'm still a member of the GDs. I'm probably going to have to deal with that when I get out. My best friend is still a GD. I don't know how he is going to feel about my becoming a Christian. Maybe I'll have to *get brought-out*, which is probably ten times worse than getting brought-in. I'll just have to face that when the time comes."

Our time together was winding down. I asked Kip what he feared most about being released from the academy. "Alcohol," he said. "It's in my family. But I'll never let that be an excuse. Drugs—maybe. Having to deal with the GDs."

"What about your anger?" I asked.

"I've always had a problem with the Fourth Commandment—with authority in general. I'm still working that out. How do you give honor to someone you just can't respect? I don't know if I'll ever be able to get back together again with my father. I know that I should. I know that a Christian honors others by forgiving others and loving them, even when they don't deserve it."

I still didn't know what made Kip's story special. I went fishing one more time. "So what's different about this time?" I asked. I was not prepared for the suddenness of his answer.

"The gospel," he said softly. "It changed my outlook on everything. It wasn't even the people at the academy, though they are good people. But the academy makes us read the Bible every day. I have learned to know Jesus. I was confirmed a few months ago. I read my Bible faithfully. I've got lots of issues to work through. But this time I have a purpose for living."

I knew the confession I had just heard came from a heart that was right with God. There might be setbacks and occasional wrong turns, but Kip would be okay. The one thing that made Kip's story so unique was the same thing that makes every Christian's story special. It is called *grace*. His young life demonstrates just how amazing God's grace is.

Let the word of Christ dwell in you richly
as you teach and admonish one another
with all wisdom, . . .

Colossians 3:16

CHAPTER SIX

ELEVENTH HOUR

There's something about fire that can penetrate a boy's soul. He is captivated by its potential to warm and heal or drawn to its power to ravage everything in its path. Fire means a lot of things to a lot of people, but what does it mean to a boy of, say . . . 11? At that age who of us could say what anything meant or explain why we did what we did? I certainly couldn't. One day I was a normal kid; the next, a pyromaniac.

Most of my friends were bad actors. But they were into crimes and habits far less harmful than firebugging. This was something that grew up within me, without anyone else's influence, like some awful, uncontrollable monster.

Do you remember the giddy sensation that accompanies a newly found freedom? No one else's sense of morality hovers overhead. You become either freedom's master or its slave. Every child is put to this test sometime during adolescence. My parents must have felt I was old enough to be trusted at home alone. That was an error in judgment. I wasn't ready for the test.

A match, tentatively scratched against the side of a matchbox, hardly seems like forbidden fruit. But, for this excitable 11-year-old, the adrenaline rush was electric. The micro-inferno burst of raw, explosive energy was sheer magic. Then the flame quivered gently for a few seconds, modified its shape and color several times, gasped for oxygen, released a thin black line of gasses, and wisped into oblivion, the pungent aroma of burning sulfur lingering in the air for a few minutes more.

Adults tend to forget that first match. But for a child it is always a special event. Not monumental. Not even memorable. Just special.

There was heat too—enough to set the house and everything in it ablaze. I let my fingers hover above the flame, moving slowly enough to feel the warmth but not close enough to cause any pain. It made me even more aware of the dangerous potential. This too was part of the game. Or rather, it *was* the whole game. A fantasy isn't worth pursuing unless there is danger in it. It was the risk, the arrogant, defiant, self-determining morality of those moments that made my fire rituals so alluring.

I raised the stakes, burning larger quantities of combustible materials. I courted tragedy. Took fewer precautions. Pilfered more matches, old newspapers, flash powder, even gunpowder. The monster was loose and roaming at large.

I'm not sure when my parents became aware of what was going on in their basement. The acrid smell of burning sulfur is hard to cover up. It was my mother who first broached the subject.

Saint Paul must have had her in mind when he wrote, "Let the word of Christ dwell in you richly as you teach and admonish one another with all wisdom" (Colossians 3:16). That was her style. She never wore religion on her sleeve like some cause; her faith ran deeper. Instead, it was as if God had spoken directly to her. "Watch me" was her unspoken message; "I will *show* you how a child of God lives." She was wisdom personified.

I was not used to seeing my mother upset. She used words like *deadly* and *dangerous* and phrases like "burn the house down" and "foolish behavior." They were said in uncharacteristic anger. But they were necessary. Given a little more time, I would undoubtedly have managed to do just that—burn the house to the ground. I might have even taken out the whole neighborhood.

My mother made her point and moved on, which, come to think of it, would have been a lot harder had I actually set the house on fire. I was punished—dish washing for about a month—an effective deterrent, though I never did see the connection between the crime and the punishment. At any rate, I never complained. I figured I probably deserved worse.

Gentle people avoid confrontation at almost any cost. Gentility and kindness are touchstones of our faith. "Blessed are the meek," said Jesus, "for they will inherit the earth" (Matthew 5:5). It's not surprising that so many of us shy away from admonishing one another, even when that is the obvious thing to do. We sometimes confuse kindness and gentility with being nonconfrontational. Admonition frequently involves intervention. Intervention implies confrontation. Most normal, well-adjusted Christians shrink from confrontation.

We also have difficulty admonishing one another because we know our own hearts so well. We look at a fellow Christian trapped in an endless cycle of sin and temptation and we say, "I'm hardly the one to admonish him or her. Am I any better?" But, without that humble and contrite spirit, all the well-intentioned admonition in the world is worthless. Who would listen? Without humility, admonition comes off as pure arrogance. That was the spirit of the Pharisees. Jesus called them whitewashed tombs. His words were meant not only as a sharp warning for the Pharisees; they were also aimed at anyone mired in self-righteousness and legalism.

Humility, then, is a necessary frame of mind for carrying out God-pleasing admonition. Jesus said that we should make sure to take the huge wooden plank out of our own eyes before attempting to remove a splinter from someone else's eye (Matthew 7:3-5; Luke 6:41,42). That's very practical advice for would-be admonishers.

At the same time, however, godly humility needs to be tempered with the confidence that we have been washed clean in the blood of the Lamb. This is one of the great paradoxes of the Christian life. We are at once humbled by our sin and confident of his forgiveness. And both are prerequisite to godly admonition.

To admonish someone is to correct that person in a way that makes him aware of the danger he is in. The Bible tells us, "[Speak] the truth in love" (Ephesians 4:15). That is another way of describing godly admonition.

68

The truth spoken of in Ephesians chapter 4 consists of two indisputable facts. The first is the fact of sin—*our* sin or, more to the point, *my* sin. This fact makes us unacceptable in God's holy presence. God hates sin. The second fact is that God has, through the work of Christ Jesus, wiped our slates clean. We are forgiven—fully. We are also fully reinstated into his divine family as though nothing ever happened to interrupt our cherished relationship. In other words, God loves us through Christ, with *no strings attached*.

But sometimes we have difficulty admitting sin. Either we don't want to give up our pet sins, or we are unable to accept our sins as a matter of fact. In either case, the end result is the same: unbelief! Without repentance, we will eventually become hardened to sin. In time, as in the case of Pharaoh (Exodus 10:1), God himself may actually confirm the hardening process.

Given that sad scenario, it is easy to see why patient admonition is such a loving act. An unbroken cycle of sin is tantamount to slow spiritual strangulation. When a friend is trapped in such a cycle, there may be only one person in a position to do anything about breaking the cycle. And you might be that person. God uses our fellowship with one another to bring an erring brother or sister face-to-face with the deadly reality of sin. The story of King David and the prophet Nathan is an example of how Christian intervention works.

David, you may recall, had committed a series of sins, including lust, adultery, deception, conspiracy, and murder. He was knee-deep in a cover-up, and, as he later admitted, he was being tormented by his guilty conscience. Although a godly man, David was stuck in denial, and his denial was directly connected to an unrepentant heart. Blatant unbelief was probably not far behind. He was approaching that point of no return in which the heart becomes so hardened that all hope for repentance is gone. But, remember, we are speaking of God's servant, David, the Lord's own anointed, *a man after God's own heart.*

In love God intervened, sending his prophet Nathan to confront David with his sin. Nathan's approach was honest and direct. He used an interactive parable to convict David (2 Samuel 12). When David finally saw the wretched condition of his own heart, he was filled with remorse.

David knew where to go with his sins. He sought pardon from his Savior-God and freedom from the burden of his guilt. The Lord reassured David that he had been forgiven and was restored to favorite-son status. In one of his most quoted psalms, David confessed, "Cleanse me with hyssop, and I will be clean; wash me, and I will be whiter than snow" (Psalm 51:7).

Measured in human terms, not all interventions lead to successful outcomes. But when we speak the truth in love, no matter what the outcome, we are carrying out God's will. Of that we can be certain.

People get caught in the revolving door of temptation and sin. It happens more often than we would like to admit. It happened in Jesus' day. He once told a wealthy young man, who was caught up in the sin of greed, to sell all that he had and give the money to the poor. The man turned and sadly walked away. The man had failed Jesus' test.

But there were successes also. To a Samaritan woman, Jesus pointed out that her current relationship with a man was not a God-pleasing one. There was a pattern of wrongheaded behavior in her relationships. She had been married five times.

This time she hadn't even bothered to marry the guy. Jesus' words cut with the precision of a surgeon's knife, and the way to repentance was opened.

To another woman, an adulteress whom Jesus had just rescued from being stoned, he simply said, "Go now and leave your life of sin" (John 8:11).

When I first met Mick, we had almost nothing in common. Mick had fought in the Korean War. I had not served in the armed forces. Mick was rugged, hearty, and hardened. The things he experienced in Korea had toughened him and given him a huge sense of bravado. He had soldiered with men who would stand up to the devil. Now he was employed in the building trades, a crew boss. I was in education—learning even as I taught—learning to be patient and sensitive to the feelings of others. Mick was 15 years older than I. He took an adversarial position on just about everything and made enemies easily. His style was all rough around the edges, leathery and gritty, earthy, unpredictable, spontaneous, cunning. There was a whole laundry list of reasons why a friendship between us should have been impossible. Yet, in spite of our differences, we got along well. Perhaps the bonding agent was our Christian faith.

Mick was married to a fine Christian woman named Myra. The two loved children but had none of their own until they adopted two little girls.

Myra and I were teaching associates. We worked together well. Soon my wife and I were socializing with Myra and Mick on a regular basis. Mick had an abundance of interesting stories to tell, and Myra was a gracious hostess. We often laughed and ate and drank late into the night. Our friendship deepened over the years.

One night, after Mick and Myra's adopted children had grown to adulthood, I got a call from one of their daughters. The conversation was vague and awkward. She tried to remain calm but without success. Had I noticed a problem in her family?

The question didn't register. What kind of problem? With whom? Why was she asking me? I told her I wasn't sure if I understood what she was talking about.

She started over. "Do you think my father has a problem?"

There was an uncomfortable pause. I still didn't get it.

"Do you think he drinks too much?" she finally asked bluntly.

I wasn't sure if this was an accusation or if I was being asked to arbitrate some kind of family dispute. I wasn't about to commit myself to an answer that would lock me into a position when I didn't know what lay behind the question. Besides, Mick was my friend. Among friends there is a code of loyalty: you defend one another at all costs. Mick liked his beer. No one would argue that. But so do lots of other people. Life was a never-ending party for Mick. That was one of the things I liked about him. He never allowed himself to become too serious about anything. But as I gathered my wits, I realized I might be too close to Mick to see the truth. What if there really was a problem and I just wasn't able to be objective enough to see it? What if Mick was so good at hiding a drinking problem that his friends couldn't see it? What kind of friend would I be to turn my back on him when he needed me most? I decided to listen.

It took several weeks for that first conversation with Mick's daughter to sink in. I became more observant. I asked questions, always trying to put the best construction on what I heard. I learned that Mick apparently could make it through a work day without having a drink. But if he didn't get home from work soon enough, his hands would begin to shake, and he would become very irritable. He needed a few beers to calm down. Then he would slowly work his way through a couple of six packs and a few shots of brandy over the next few hours.

Weekends were worse. The party started early Saturday morning and lasted through Sunday night.

I also learned of times that Mick had blacked out while driving his grandchildren to piano lessons — of near misses at intersections — of failing to stop at red lights — of temporarily losing control of the car. He was an accident waiting to happen.

Mick's daughter found two people at her church who had experience doing drug and alcohol interventions among teens. Even though Mick was far from being a teenager, they volunteered to help and immediately began planning a formal intervention. The phone call I had received was one of the first contacts made in the hope of building a team of Mick's friends and family members. I finally agreed to join the effort, though I had conflicting feelings over the intervention process. My struggle revolved around the sense that I was somehow betraying a personal trust by conspiring with others behind Mick's back.

The intervention group was finally complete. Besides the two intervention specialists, the team consisted of the daughter of Mick and Myra who had called me, another friend of the family, myself, one of Mick's fellow workers, his employer, and his pastor — eight people in all. We met several times over the course of the next two months to talk through the things we planned to say to Mick on the day of the intervention. We wrote mock letters in order to put the right words together and discussed the order in which we would confront Mick. The team leader explained that Mick's health insurance company had agreed to cover rehab costs. Mick's employer told us that he would promise to hold Mick's job open, contingent upon his sobriety. Arrangements had been made with a local drug rehabilitation facility to receive Mick in a 30-day, full-care program.

The team tried to convince Myra that she was a key person to Mick's recovery. In the end, she declined to join the team, fearing that such a role would put her marriage in jeopardy. She loved Mick too much to risk losing that. But she recognized Mick's problem. And she understood that, for years with her silence, she had been giving Mick permission to drink himself to death. More than anyone, Myra wanted Mick to be the whole, caring, functional human being she had married. So she packed Mick's things in a suitcase and hid it away in a closet until the day of the intervention. It was not a small thing for her to do.

We decided to hold the intervention late on a workday afternoon when Mick was not under the influence. The meeting was to take place at Mick's job site during an afternoon break. His employer found a room that would provide security and privacy.

Intervention has been referred to as *tough love*. It is that in the extreme. Stepping into an intervention is like going to war. Two opposing wills fiercely contend for control. It is the raw stuff of human confrontation. The risks are enormous; the tensions huge. Relationships are on the line. Once you have committed, there is no turning back.

Mick's face turned ashen the moment he met our little group in the hallway. We asked him to step into a nearby room. There were no cordial greetings. We sat down in complete silence. The intervention leader introduced himself to Mick and explained why we were there. "Your friends," said the leader, "care for you too much to watch you waste the rest of your life without speaking up." Then each of us took a turn at speaking from the heart—speaking the truth in love. The words came out halting and stammered, each sentence a labor of love. A few members of the group read written messages. Some had memorized little soliloquies. Scripture texts were quoted. Prayers were recited. The purpose of all the careful planning had been to eliminate surprises and avoid unexpected barriers. In actuality, none of us had any way of knowing what to expect.

Mick stiffened. He took an expanding ruler out of his work pants and started beating it angrily in the palm of his hand. His adrenaline was surging. His voice quivered when he spoke, filled with a mixture of rage and shame. Finally, he exploded: "This is bogus bullshit! What are you guys trying to do to me? You call yourselves friends?" He slammed the ruler hard into his palm for emphasis.

Our emotional reserves were on low battery. The progress was agonizingly slow; the tension, unnerving. Two and a half hours later, the intervention was still in search of resolution. Mick showed no sign of weakening, though he had long ago realized this was no party.

We had intentionally positioned Mick's pastor in front of the door—standing. He was a big, husky fellow. During another angry outburst, Mick bolted across the room, threatening to leave. When he realized who blocked the door and heard a calm voice encouraging him to relax, he gave up the effort and returned to his seat.

We started over, explaining the implications that his addiction had for our friendships. We also spoke of the consequences his alcoholism had on his family—of the dangers to his grandchildren. We explained how it was undermining his relationship with his God and was therefore placing his eternal future in jeopardy. Impatient, angry, Mick listened.

He had questions. What about his job? What about the costs of a recovery program? The detailed forethought that had gone into our effort was beginning to make more sense now.

Mick's hands began to shake. "I'd better get home. Myra's waiting for me. Maybe tomorrow." We ignored his protest and pressed on, knowing the torment of withdrawal had to get worse before Mick could begin to get better.

In the end, Mick agreed to check himself into the rehab facility that same afternoon. His other daughter met us in the hallway, suitcase in hand. On the way to the parking lot, Mick's pastor said a short prayer with him. Then his daughters drove him to the rehab center. The battle for Mick's life was just beginning.

Be devoted to one another
in brotherly love.

Romans 12:10

CHAPTER SEVEN

GERALDINE

The fall of my 12th year was a record breaker. My voice was beginning to have a rich, baritone quality. I had learned how to shoot a jump shot. My circle of friends was widening. High school was somewhere off in a distant haze. And my shadow was finally beginning to lengthen in the October sun. Life could not have been more perfect.

Then, in the back row of the church balcony one Reformation Sunday, during the school choir's singing of the second verse of "A Mighty Fortress Is Our God," I experienced what I can only describe as an adolescent epiphany. Such events fix themselves in one's memory, suspended in time. That is how I recall the moment when my right hand gently nudged Geraldine Grundman's left hand, and our two hands stuck together in a lather of sweat and white-hot emotion. She looked straight ahead—singing, flushed. I stood there dazed, recalculating my life's priorities.

It was her aloof, free spirit that first attracted my attention. She hated her name. Her friends all called her Gerry. I teased her, calling her Geraldine. She was one year my senior—a full head taller, soft and pastel, religious to a fault, smart, gloriously endowed—a goddess of virtue and beauty. She was everything a 12-year-old boy might dream of in another human being.

Adults forget those grand firsts in the formation of a complete emotional spectrum. When a 12-year-old discovers that members of the opposite sex are real people, capable of reciprocal relationships, it opens a whole new dimension in life. This was not mature love, but it was every bit as urgent and exuberant. I soared, ecstatic in the notion that I could care so deeply about another person. Nothing else mattered. School wasn't a burden; it represented more time to be with *her*. I walked *her* to a bus stop 16 blocks in the opposite direction from my house. Then she would intentionally miss a bus to give us more time to tease each other.

My day-to-day existence became surreal. I operated somewhere in the ether of romantic fantasy. In one week I lost a set of house keys and a ten-dollar bill. My school assignments went unfinished or forgotten. Nothing else mattered to me. Geraldine was my new obsession, and I was her . . . I wasn't sure what I was to her. I was hoping it was something like baseball or basketball had once been to me.

I counted the minutes until I would see her again, wrote poetry to her, read and reread every note she had ever passed to me in class. I adored her; studied her. What gum flavor did she chew? Why did she write her messages in that fluorescent green ink? What made her smell so good? Every waking moment was devoted to thinking about *her*.

Love can be a frightening thing to a 12-year-old. There are demands—cash to finance daily visits to the soda fountain—scheduling dilemmas, social pressures, parental inquiries, sibling ridicule, and challenges.

I learned there were no rules to this game. My friend Mark was the first guy to horn in on my claim. Geraldine found herself attracted to his winning smile. I knew this because she told me it was so. And my instincts told me she was accurate in her own assessment. But Mark lacked a certain savoir faire. With wit and clever maneuvering, I managed to hold him off for a week or two. Nevertheless, I could see the handwriting on the wall. Geraldine's interest in me was beginning to wane.

It was Leroy who would eventually take my place. He was athletic, fun-loving, always making people laugh. He was also two years older than I and in high school.

The end came quickly. In four weeks my first dance with romance was over. Only later did I realize the depth of my emotional investment. Geraldine and I had become something more than friends or casual acquaintances. Virgin emotions had been explored. I had discovered the passion of being thoroughly (if also immaturely) committed to another human being. It was a significant step forward on the learning curve that teaches us the value of human devotion.

Devotion seems to be one of those "for one another" abstractions that is not only difficult to implement but almost impossible to define. Just how does one human being become devoted to another?

In Old Testament times, the utensils and vessels used in temple rites had to be dedicated to that singular purpose. Once purified through a simple ceremony, such implements were permanently set aside for service in Yahweh's house, never to be used for anything else. From that moment on, their only reason for existing, common as they were, was to bring honor and glory to God's holy name. Perhaps the apostle Paul had such focus in mind when he urged Christians, "Be devoted to one another in brotherly love" (Romans 12:10).

Our devotion to one another is one more example of a gospel miracle. In sin, our attention is directed self-ward. But when God's Holy Spirit changes our hearts through faith in Jesus, we can become so zealously preoccupied with someone else's need that we are willing to forego some of our own needs for that person's sake.

The Bible is filled with wonderful examples of such selfless devotion. David and Jonathan, we are told, were knit together in brotherly devotion. Ruth's tender dedication to an embittered mother-in-law named Naomi stands as a model to be emulated by all Christians. And the fictional good Samaritan of Jesus' familiar parable serves as a powerful example of Christian sacrifice directed even toward a complete stranger.

Sometimes we do not so readily recognize our opportunities to be devoted to someone else's welfare. When was the last time you saw a guy lying in the middle of the road, bleeding to death, naked, fighting for his life? (If you did, you'd know exactly what to do, right?) It doesn't happen that way very often. Our daily opportunities aren't always so dramatic, or even so obvious. When an opportunity arises, we may decide to pass, hoping for a better one to come along. Furthermore, these opportunities always seem to arrive at the most inconvenient times, intruding into our lives when they are least welcome. We'd be glad to help out as long as it fits our schedule and, then, only if we have some control over the limits of our commitment.

Sometimes we are faced with so many opportunities we become paralyzed with indecision. At such moments, it may be necessary to apply triage—to prioritize—and then get to work.

Sometimes our own judgment gets in the way. Like the man who came to Jesus, we wrestle with the question "Who is my neighbor?" Our all too frequent answer to that question is that no *neighbor* of ours would be so foolish as to wander down such a dangerous, lonely, crime-infested highway. The sinful nature within us takes over. It argues that someone who obviously has not walked the straight and narrow doesn't really deserve our help. Logic tells us he brought it upon himself with his own foolish living. Now he is receiving his just reward. Why interfere with divine justice? We forget that Jesus gave no background information whatsoever about why the man was traveling that dangerous highway.

Sometimes we are ready to grab an opportunity but are totally at a loss about what to do. So we remain frozen in inaction. God provides us with options even then.

Have you heard the little quip "If there is nothing more that you can do, there's more praying to be done"? There's wisdom in those words. We *can* do something, even when we are unsure about what needs to be done. We can pray.

To many people today, prayer has become a cliché. The secular world has denigrated prayer, demeaned it, and demoted it to the status of a myth. Unbelievers really don't take it seriously. And why should they? Unbelievers have no practical experience with prayer's unlimited power. To an unbeliever, it's all hearsay. No unbeliever has ever really talked to God in prayer because unbelievers do not have access to the Father's throne.

Among Christians, however, prayer is (or at least should be) taken very seriously. In prayer we can step up to God's throne and make a real difference. You and I know prayer's miraculous power. Jesus has promised that our Father in heaven will hear every word and will then act on our behalf.

We may take prayer for granted. We may occasionally forget. And sometimes we may doubt that God will keep his promise to answer our prayers. But prayer is always there for us to use—an effective, powerful, reliable, responsive tool for getting things done.

Unfortunately, our first inclination is to use prayer to gather in God's blessings for ourselves. That's an innately human approach. But our prayers demonstrate that we still remember who the giver of all good things really is. And God surely wants us to pray for the things we want and need.

But the prayer life of a Christian is also quite selfless. Christ Jesus, working in our new-man hearts, is changing us—perfecting us. Our new-man focus gradually matures in a way that turns our attention away from self toward others. This new focus is especially sensitive to those who are really in need. And that might very well include our sworn enemies.

Imagine that! Would your sworn enemy accept help from you? Unlikely, isn't it. Yet, in prayer, God gives us a way to live for one another—even those who are committed to hating and despising us. Even if they reject our outward expressions of kindness, we can still pray for them (Romans 12:21). Our prayers may be the only remaining way for us to put our love for them into action.

With God's gift of prayer, our devotion for one another then extends to virtually every living person on the face of the earth.

The October skies were dark and foreboding. Huddled in the corridor of a dreary, old funeral home, six children, ages 3 to 13, considered their future. They were trying to sort out their young lives; they were trying to determine who was going to live where.

The children's mother was a hopeless coke addict. In her place, their Gramma Coretta-Jean had cared for all six of them from birth. Now Gramma was gone.

No panic or urgency drove their discussion. In fact, the six seemed to accept their circumstances rather calmly. The chaos of chemical addiction shatters families, but it teaches individuals to take life's curve balls as they come. The older ones understood their plight. For most of their young lives, they had been living with the realization that this day would come too soon. Corey, the second oldest, told his five siblings, "We belong to the state of Wisconsin now."

Coretta-Jean had brought 15 children besides their mother into the world. All 16 of her children had long ago given in to the ways of the street. Not one could be trusted to take on the responsibility of raising six kids. Each harbored selfish motives for claiming the children. Welfare money lay at the heart of their false benevolence.

A hearing to determine the disposition of the six children was scheduled for the Monday of Thanksgiving week. Marshall,

Coretta-Jean's half-brother, put in his own bid for keeping the children. But Marshall had bad habits of his own. He represented as great a danger to this young family as Coretta-Jean's 15 greedy adult children.

The social worker handling the case convinced the judge to suspend judgment for a week. She hoped to find a more stable, permanent home for the children. The prospects of that actually happening seemed next to impossible. Meanwhile, the six kids were ordered to remain with Marshall.

Within days Chenise, the oldest, ran away. She sensed the danger that living in the same house with Marshal presented. So she went to live with one of her aunts, who was herself not much older than Chenise. But the aunt's home setting wasn't much safer or more stable than Marshall's. Finding a way to get all six children into a safer environment was of the highest priority.

Gramma Coretta-Jean had been the only stable influence in the lives of these six youngsters. A God-fearing woman, she had cared for the children as though they were her own. Gramma taught her grandchildren to love their mother even though she had passed her crack addiction and its side effects on to five of her six offspring. Coretta-Jean sent those who were old enough for school to Immanuel Lutheran School, where she knew they would hear about their Savior. She hoped they would also have a better chance there to develop the attitudes and life skills necessary to escape the drug-infested street life of the inner city.

Word of the six orphaned children traveled quickly among the members of Coretta-Jean's church. Several members immediately volunteered to house some of the kids. Many prayers were said. Pastor Dumont told his members that the most immediate objective was to try to place each of the children into a stable environment for the remainder of that school year. He secretly hoped that permanent homes within the congregation could later be arranged through foster care or outright adoption. A new theme echoed throughout the church's halls: Sometimes it takes a church to raise a child.

The members' love took wing. A large sum of money was collected for the children's education. Church leaders invited neighboring congregations to help out. The response was overwhelming. Toys and clothing, appropriately sized for each child, were gathered. Wisconsin Lutheran High School helped organize and sponsor the event. Wisconsin Lutheran College provided dormitory space for storing the many donations. Several more families stepped forward to volunteer their homes as safe havens for one or more of the six children. By Thanksgiving Day only one of the six still needed placement. Pastor Dumont and his wife decided to ask Corey if he would like to come and stay with them.

On the day of the hearing, the children's biological mother showed up to plead her case. Some of the older children still harbored the hope that their family could be reunited with their natural mother. The judge immediately saw the futility in that. A few of the mother's siblings also showed up to stake their claim. In the end, the judge listened with great patience to a plan worked out by Pastor Dumont and the children's attorney ad litem. The miracle everyone was praying for had, in fact, taken place. Pastor Dumont was able to demonstrate to the judge that all of the children had stable homes in which they might now be placed. The judge ruled in favor of the people of Immanuel Lutheran Church who had worked so hard to find suitable homes for all six children.

After the hearing, Pastor Dumont went to Marshal's house to tell the children about the court's decision. There he gathered up whatever belongings he could find, which consisted of not much more than a bag full of cockroach-infested clothes. Within the hour he had delivered five of the children to their new homes. Upon finally arriving at the Dumont residence, Corey hailed Mrs. Dumont warmly with the greeting "Hi, Mom, your son is home."

*Let us consider how we may spur one
another on toward love and good deeds.*

Hebrews 10:24

CHAPTER EIGHT

Twenty-three Baptisms

Milwaukee was a leading industrial center in the fifties. Stronger union shops meant that factory jobs paid better wages than agricultural jobs in the South. The industrial growth generated by the Second World War meant new economic opportunity for impoverished southern sharecroppers. African-Americans migrated into the industrial northern cities of Detroit, Chicago, and Milwaukee in record numbers.

As neighborhoods rapidly changed, many white urban churches struggled to survive. Congregations were faced with having to decide whether they were going to continue to carry on their ministry in the central city or relocate to the outskirts of town. They wrestled with questions about economic security, and they wondered about the stresses connected with a racially mixed membership.

Many congregations exercised the option to move their churches out, closer to the majority of the members. Our little

Lutheran church decided to stay. Following a meeting of the voters' assembly, my father proudly announced to the family that our church was committed to staying and serving the inner-city community no matter what the consequences of that decision might be. But, he added, we should be expecting a lot of changes in our church and in our neighborhood.

It didn't take long to find out what my father meant. Racial tensions soon rose to a volatile level in the community. A decade later those would tensions explode in violent race riots.

In spite of all the change, our congregation remained steadfast and up to the challenges that such changes represented. Almost immediately, our little church was reaching out with the gospel to a changing community in new and different ways. Though only ten years old, even I felt the excitement.

A few weeks after the deciding vote, our Sunday worship began with the announcement that the service would be a little different from the usual fare. We were about to celebrate a "special event." With that, the congregation watched the approach of 23 men, women, and children—all strangers and every one of them black. They marched straight to the baptismal font. Then, one by one, they leaned over the little pool. The pastor repeated the same words 23 times, as his cupped hand poured water over their heads. After the half-hour ceremony, the strangers were introduced to the congregation. We applauded, stepping out of our pews to greet the new people as though they were long-lost members of our own family.[3]

That morning my Sunday school teacher asked us to invite our unchurched friends to Sunday school the next week. Her request was problematic for me. I knew the religious affiliations of every kid in my neighborhood. Most rarely attended church, but they all claimed membership in some local church or synagogue. I didn't know anyone who was "unchurched."

Then I remembered Roberto. Though our paths crossed almost daily, we seldom talked because we attended different schools. Our only real contact came in winter, when we occasionally lobbed friendly snowballs at each other, and in spring, when we gambled for baseball cards. It was a boyish kinship. Judging by his vocabulary, I was pretty sure Roberto was *unchurched*. In those days most of us still believed that religious people didn't use vulgar language or curse in public. Roberto's vocabulary could blister paint.

My invitation was terse. So was his response. "Okay," was all he said.

On Sunday morning I climbed a narrow, cluttered stairwell to get to the apartment where Roberto lived with his mother. He was waiting for me, dressed in a clean, white shirt and tie. His mother, who barely spoke English, greeted me, "Buenos días."

I buenos-díased her back. Then she kissed Roberto on the cheek and sent the two of us on our way.

That is all I can recall of that childhood memory. I wish I could report more. I wish I could say that we became lifelong friends. I wish I could tell people that Roberto was baptized and his mother started going to church. It didn't happen. At least I don't know that it happened.

I don't recall either whether Roberto and I associated much after that. We probably lobbed a few friendly snowballs at each other in winter and gambled for baseball cards in the spring. However, this brief experience did show me that there are plenty of opportunities to touch the lives of people who don't know the Savior. Sometimes we just need a little nudge.

We plant; God grants. As workers in a harvest that spans all of human history, we are tireless in spurring one another on to carry out Jesus' commission. The work is ours; the results are his. We plant; God grants.

The gospel travels like the wind. It takes wing according to the divine will of God's Holy Spirit. Jesus said, "The wind blows wherever it pleases. You hear its sound, but you cannot tell where it comes from or where it is going" (John 3:8). It does not always travel in a straight line. Nor does it move according to the whims and wishes of men. We can't predict where or how the Spirit will work his miracles of faith. We do not always get to see the end results of our planting efforts. And we certainly have no control over the success of the harvest. *We merely plant; God grants.*

But even in the simple act of planting the gospel seed, we sometimes manage to bungle the process and frustrate the plan. Most of the time, we err on the side of being far too conservative in our efforts to share the gospel. Often we are paralyzed with fear. Occasionally we mistake caution for good stewardship of the gospel. Or we apply the risk-management principles so prevalent in today's business world instead of throwing caution to the wind and engaging in entrepreneurial evangelism. We forget Jesus' promise to be with us in all of our outreach endeavors. Instead of spurring one another on with gospel encouragement, we warn one another of the dire consequences of overreaching our resources. We remind one another that new and untried directions for spreading God's truth come with monumental risks for failure. The end result, all too often, is that we shrink from carrying out the work that Jesus called us to do; we do nothing.

For centuries a dominant force in Western culture has been man's ability to dream. Mankind's vision for a better world has touched virtually every aspect of human endeavor, from medicine and technology and the world's economy to the political landscape. Life, as we know it, would be unrecognizable without the new ideas that have found their way into our culture over the last four centuries. Columbus dreamed of discovering and conquering new lands. Implementing that dream involved monumental risks. The framers of the American Constitution demonstrated that entrepreneurial ability to dream when they connected human freedoms to the rule of law.

Christians have also done their share of dreaming. The dream of God's people is for a world that knows its Savior with great intimacy and love. The dream is not without risks either. Luther's break with Rome, for example—his preachment of God's love as it flows to humankind in grace alone, through faith alone, and in biblical revelation alone—represented an investment of astounding human risk and remarkable courage.

One of the most disturbing attitudes permeating the thinking of our culture today is the proposition that dreaming—the kind of dreaming that requires risk—is a waste of time and energy. One observer of contemporary life has said that today's young people have stopped dreaming altogether. That's scary!

Most adults have a difficult time understanding how this could possibly be. Dreaming of a better future is innate. The results of mankind's dreams during this last century speak for themselves. Who can ignore the advances in modern medicine, the profound developments in communication technology, and the astounding strides made in understanding our universe and the workings of the human brain? Still, today's young people have concluded that, for all the promise of modern history, we are still beset by wars, injustice, poverty, and disease. To them the innovations aimed at making life better have not delivered on their promises. As a result, an entire generation is in danger of getting mired in a swamp of pessimism.

For many young people today, life has no real meaning. To a greater degree, this generation has stopped idealizing the future. It is a generation that has quit being optimistic. Our young people today see their world as a very fragile place. They see an environment that is increasingly in peril and a population that is quickly outgrowing the planet's natural resources. Dark clouds threaten. Acid rain. Ozone depletion. Deforestation. These topics permeate school curriculum materials. Among young people there is a growing sentiment that we are living in an age that will eventually come to some terrible, universal apocalyptic end. Stanley Grenz, a well-known author on contemporary culture, writes, "The Postmodern generation is convinced that life on the earth is fragile. They believe that the survival of humankind is now at stake."[4]

The games our young people play, the music they enjoy, and the films and videos they watch are often constructed around apocalyptic themes. They are convinced some secular Armageddon is inevitable.

What irony! The unbelieving world is itself arriving at a conclusion foretold long ago in the pages of Scripture. What an opportunity to reach out to those lost souls for whom the end is already in sight! When the church becomes too careful and cautious with the gospel, it is bypassing opportunities to reach out to young people who are desperate with pessimism and fear.

The church's business, remember, is to *go, preach, teach,* and *make disciples.* But we sometimes act as if preaching the gospel is the same thing as betting the heavenly ranch. We are intimidated by the risks and thus become overly careful about managing our ministry ventures.

One area in which we have not always been good stewards of the resources God has given to his church is the way in which we put the lay members of our churches to work in the harvest fields. A friend illustrated the problem with a recent experience.

I should preface this story by observing that both my friend and his wife are fine examples of faithful, intelligent lay Christians. They are Bible literate and have a special zeal for sharing the gospel with those who do not yet know Jesus.

My friends were looking for a way to do some outreach work away from their home congregation. They were excited to learn of an opportunity to teach vacation Bible school in an inner-city congregation. They agreed to cover all the travel costs and motel expenses. They arranged a week's vacation for their adventure.

When they arrived, the pastor welcomed them warmly and showed them around. Then it was on to a crash course in teaching methodology and a brief program orientation.

Soon, however, my friends discovered that very few of the congregation's lay members were participating in the program. The actual hands-on Bible teaching was clearly perceived as the pastor's bailiwick. For all practical purposes, my friends were relegated to the positions of cookie servers, Kool-Aid mixers, and arts-and-crafts aides. Ideas for improving the program by involving more people in actual Bible teaching received a cool reception. The rationale my friend and his wife heard from church members generally implied that the pastor was obviously better trained for preaching and teaching God's Word than they. Letting less-well-trained people share the Word seemed like risky business. One member argued, "You put your best hitters at the plate." The suggestion that more opportunities *at the plate* could improve the whole team's batting average was met with cool indifference. There was much more risk that false doctrine might somehow creep into the church if lay members became too involved in handling God's Word.

This anecdote may seem an unfair criticism of the pastor. Actually it probably points to a weakness in the way both our clergy and laity approach ministry. One certainly has to wonder where all the lay members of that congregation were. Didn't they have an obligation to point out to their spiritual leader that gospel ministry is everybody's work? Didn't they have a responsibility to examine their spiritual gifts to determine how and where they could serve? Then again, one has to wonder also why they were not being trained, encouraged, and challenged to carry out a gospel ministry of their own. Why weren't they eager to let the name of Jesus pass through their lips as well?

More than likely the answer to that question has something to do with *fear.* Jesus exposed the old-Adam fear that so often still lurks even in a Christian's heart by telling a story to his followers:

A man entrusted his property to three of his servants while he went away on business. To one he gave five talents. To another he gave two talents. And to the third he entrusted one talent. In the master's absence, each servant was instructed to handle a sum in keeping with his ability.

On his return, the master called in the servants to review their work. The servant who had been given five talents had put the money to work and gained five more talents. The second servant had likewise invested the money and doubled the investment. But the third servant explained that he had dug a hole and buried the one talent. His reason? He knew that the master was a hard man, harvesting where he had not sewn and gathering where he had not scattered. *The servant was afraid* and went out and hid his talent in the ground. (Matthew 25)

The master's response shows that Jesus was pointing to unbelievers who use fear as an excuse for misusing and abusing the gifts God has given them. Every one of us still has an unbelieving sinful nature that uses fear as an excuse for neglecting the special trust our heavenly Master has given to us.

Some would argue that God has simply not gifted all his people in the same way, that there are many lay members who just don't feel they have the gift to speak to someone else about the Savior's love for them. The argument infers that personal evangelism is just another gift, like playing an organ, operating sound equipment, handing out bulletins, or making a casserole for a fellowship meal. In the wake of such an argument, lay members often mistakenly conclude that Bible talk is generally reserved as the pastor's work, since that is obviously his gift.

The gift for sharing the simple gospel message with others goes far beyond many of the other gifts we have received. It is a privilege for all Christians to tell someone else about Jesus. It is a gift that is worth encouraging and practicing.

Many pastors work hard at equipping their members for such opportunities. Many church leaders realize that, for the spiritual good of their lay members, the programs of the church need to provide more opportunities for hands-on sharing of Bible truth.

On the other hand, I have heard too many variations of my friend's story to be optimistic. In too many congregations, lay members would prefer to blend in with the furniture. We have entertained too many excuses, from clergy and laity alike, justifying why the pastor ends up doing all the heavy spiritual lifting. I have observed lay members intensely excited by a new idea for reaching people with the gospel only to have cold water thrown on their enthusiasm because they didn't speak with the authority of ordination. Whether it happens intentionally or unintentionally is not the issue. Whenever we leave lay members to infer that faith-talk is better left to the professionals, we stifle the gospel's free flow.

Every man, woman, and child among us can enjoy the privilege of telling someone else about Jesus. We are all part of Christ's royal priesthood. There is no other priesthood. God gave this dream to all his New Testament people. We can excuse neither the laziness or complacency of the laity nor the ill-advised usurping of their ministry joy. To do so is to limit the work force and douse water on the Spirit's fiery gift. Ultimately, to risk-manage the gospel's spread by limiting the workforce to those who have been called, ordained, installed, or inducted is to doubt Jesus' own promise to be with us and to work through his Word as we carry out his Great Commission.

Like everything else in a Christian's life, our dreams are sanctified; they are made new by our faith in Jesus. They are wrapped in God's promise to be with us, to guide us, and to direct us. There is real power in that promise. With it "we demolish arguments and every pretension that sets itself up against the knowledge of God, and we take captive every thought to make it obedient to Christ" (2 Corinthians 10:5).

The gospel is like the wind. We cannot control the jet streams and ocean currents of the Spirit's movement. We can only dream that God will use each one of us to accomplish his purpose. When we trust in God's promises, even the most radical ideas can be made obedient to Christ. With confidence in his promises, we can risk everything for his sake.

When our children were approaching their teens, I offered to take them to a local riding stable for an afternoon ride in the countryside. I had learned to ride in my teens. Now I wanted my kids to have the same experience. And, of course, I was eager to show them my equestrian skills, modest as they were.

As luck would have it, the only three horses left in the stable turned out to be a palomino named Bill, a pinto named Bullet, and a swaybacked bay nag named Feather. In deference to my kids, I volunteered to saddle up Feather.

For the next three hours, Feather and I meandered wearily down the trail, bringing up the rear and stopping at every clump of withered grass along the way. My equestrian skills not withstanding, I did just about everything I could to get Feather focused on moving in a forward direction. I cajoled her; I sweet-talked her; I nudged her gently. Nothing worked.

The trail boss came back to the end of the line every now and then to check on us. "Feather needs a firm hand," he said. "We think she is going deaf. Talk to her in a louder voice."

I did. Feather dropped her head to search for some more grass along the trail. My kids looked on, doubting I had ever been near a horse in my life.

The one thing I had not tried as yet was a good sharp kick as though I had shiny silver spurs attached to my tennis shoes. Maybe that would get Feather's attention. I reared back with all my strength and let Feather know who was boss. With that she lurched forward, bolted down the slope, and shot through a little thicket with me hanging on desperately to the saddle horn. My hat flew in one direction; my glasses, in another. Soon Feather and I found ourselves at the head of the pack, careening for the barn. My kids followed at a distance, finally impressed with their father's riding prowess.

Whenever I am thinking about the work that needs to be done in God's kingdom, I remember Feather. The author of the book of Hebrews wrote, "Let us consider how we may spur one another on toward love and good deeds" (10:24). *Spur one another on* strikes us an odd choice of words, until we have met someone in God's church who functions like Feather.

Most of us need a sharp spurring every now and then just to get us moving. There's work to be done, souls to be won. We each have a stake in that effort. We all share in that evangelical dream. Sometimes it is necessary to help our fellow Christians reach their potential by pointing them to the nearest mirror. They may need to take a long, hard, introspective look at their attitudes about risk and their personal commitment to doing real gospel ministry. That goes for lay members and clergy alike.

Eric was not a particularly good student. He frequently came to class unprepared. Eric didn't get along well with his classmates either. He was always on the defensive—argumentative, hostile. It wasn't so much that Eric didn't care about having friends. He just lacked the tools to attack life from a positive angle. It was hard for others to like him.

Eric's home life wasn't much better. His mom was in her second marriage, and Eric's relationship with his stepfather was strained.

On the other hand, Eric's faith was stalwart. He loved his Savior. He knew his eternal future. He read and memorized Bible passages with enthusiasm. He attended church regularly with his mother. And he wasn't afraid to share his personal convictions with his peers. Not that anyone was listening.

Late one evening I received a phone call from Eric's stepfather. I had only met his stepdad once, since Mr. Heisel was not a member of our church. Most of my dealings had been with Eric's mother, but I had seen Mr. Heisel in action with one of our other teachers. My observations then had left me feeling that he was a bitter, pessimistic, negative, ornery man. I had already concluded that he was a contributing factor in Eric's programmed-for-failure profile.

The phone conversation was one-sided and intense. Eric's faith was apparently just as active around the house as it was in the classroom. But his style came off more like evangelical antagonism.

Mr. Heisel said that he was fed up with Eric's *blankety-blank* evangelizing at home. Either I put a stop to Eric's *bleaping* nagging about him not attending church, or he was going to pull Eric out of our school. My only accomplishment during the 20-minute tirade was to get Mr. Heisel to agree to meet with me over the matter. I considered that a minor victory.

Mr. Heisel refused to shake my hand as he and his wife stepped into my office. He also refused to participate in the prayer I customarily used to begin a consultation. Eric's mom and I prayed together as Eric's stepfather looked on impatiently. Even as I said the amen, I could feel the temperature in the room rising.

There was no beating around the bush with Mr. Heisel. He cursed and berated the school, Christian education, the church, the children in my classroom, teachers, the clergy, Eric, me, God, and his wife. He did this in no particular order, with equal fervor, and without a morsel of reverence for God or man.

After an hour's harangue, Mr. Heisel began to run out of steam. He was starting to become redundant, and I was beginning to resign myself to the possibility that I might lose Eric as my student. At the moment I felt rather ambivalent regarding that prospect.

Bringing a parent-teacher consultation to closure is an art. There was no point in prolonging the session, so I casually moved across the room to open the door—a not-so-subtle hint that we were done, even if *done* meant that we were at an impasse. I was tired of the verbal abuse. I was tired of not being given a chance to defend Eric or myself. I was just tired.

Then I heard Mr. Heisel mumbling something strangely out of character. At first it didn't register—something about being *too rough around the edges to fit into our pastor's blankety-blank adult confirmation instruction class.* I had the sensation of gears stripping in my head. Instinct led me to retrace my steps to the protection of my desk. A few probing questions revealed a load of insecurity and self-abasement in Mr. Heisel. He hated himself. He hated his life. He was afraid and lonely. Tears welled up in his eyes and moistened his cheeks. He was missing something that Eric had. That much he knew. He had no idea what it was or how he might get it for himself.

I said very little. Mostly I observed God's Spirit working a powerful miracle of repentance in a proud and stubborn heart. Ten minutes into the restart, Eric's stepfather agreed to go to church regularly with his family and to begin attending an adult instruction class. I was speechless, awed by the unpredictability of the wind.

I myself am convinced, my brothers,

that you yourselves are full of goodness,

complete in knowledge and competent

to instruct one another.

Romans 15:14

CHAPTER NINE

WINTER CITY

Life in the inner city can be depressing. The streets are narrow and dirty; the landscape, scarred with skeletons of rusted-out junkers. Living quarters are not only confining but often poorly heated and without air-conditioning. Many are infested with roaches and rodents. Drunks, addicts, prostitutes, and vagrants hang out in the vacant hulks of abandoned buildings. They shuffle through back alleys, rummaging garbage bins. Crime skulks in the darkness, searching for unwary victims. Family dysfunction, illiteracy, disease, graft, hunger, and sleaze are generally found in higher proportions here than in rural or suburban America. Poverty circles overhead like a flock of buzzards. Those without jobs wait against hope for their streak of bad luck to change. That day never arrives.

Young people dream of escaping. Their dream fades, often unrealized. For most, day-to-day existence remains in dark antithesis to the good life, which society takes great pleasure in flaunting at every turn.

The inner city is a hard place in which to live without giving up on life. It was like that when I grew up there. It hasn't changed. Then, as now, November, December, and January were the hardest months of the year for people to hang on to hope. Those sunless days only added to the city's heavy burden.

For a while, a child's imagination can find diversions from these depressing circumstances even when adults cannot. Whenever the city's first blanket of fresh snow would fall, our bleak surroundings were all but forgotten in the unexpected beauty of the newly whitened landscape. Ugly wrecks were magically transformed into sculpted works of modern art. Dingy apartments and row houses glowed with hospitality. Street litter turned into happy little gift packages waiting to be unwrapped. And dangerous back alleys were suddenly paved with a silver-white quilt of renewed hope. The impressionistic scenes left by the newly fallen snow may have been only an illusion, but to a child the effect was magical and uplifting.

The city's first snowfall often came just days before Christmas. The snow's illusions added to the wonderful mystique of the season. Powdery dustings of an inch or two blazed the way for breathtaking surprises. The miracle of snow connected well with the miracle of Jesus' arrival in Bethlehem. Everyone smiled more and laughed more. Father waited for the first snow to buy a fresh blue spruce from the tree lot. We would drag it home and ceremoniously bring it inside, where it occupied a quarter of the living room. Some of us trimmed. Some wrapped gifts. We all listened to carols on the hi-fi while Mother busied herself in the kitchen, baking cookies.

Christmas Eve generated more commotion and anticipation than any other day of the year. The gift exchange was always a time for secrets and special surprises. But it was the children's service in church that outdistanced everything else for sheer excitement. What a proud moment—standing shoulder to shoulder with my friends before a church full of parents and grandparents to recite Saint Luke's account of the first Christmas! Once a year we had the privilege of *teaching* others about the baby Jesus. Even the adults listened. They loved the story as much as we did. Like the first snow that covered the wretched landscape, it brightened our neighborhood. Only this was real enlightenment—a story so profoundly powerful it could change even the miserable lives of people living in the inner city.

Much of what we see in the world today is enough to drive us to despair. Some view the ghastly tragedy of students shooting students as a harbinger of more senseless, widespread bloodletting in American communities. Urban street gangs have been suggested as a foreshadowing of futuristic society. Alarming? Yes. Hyperboles for a troubled age? Perhaps. Nevertheless, it is hard even for Christians to remain enthusiastic about the future when society is in such turmoil.

One of the most disturbing aspects of prevailing thought is the frontal assault on reality and truth. People are confused. And, though it is neither logical nor reasonable, their faulty perception has become a kind of reality—a truth, if you will, of its own. For many people, whatever their feelings are at any given moment establishes what is truth for them. Movies and other various media have contributed largely to this false way of seeing the universe. As the lines between fantasy and reality blur, perception is quickly becoming the only *reality* that matters.

Truth, the reality of life as we know it, is vital to our understanding of ourselves and the universe in which we live. We are not figments of someone else's imagination. God is not a figment of our imaginations—neither is Satan or heaven or hell. The simple truth is that these are indeed realities.

Truth is of major importance in a Christian's approach to life. Human truth, even the truth of the most respected thinkers, may fall by the wayside, but God's truth remains whole and intact. Isaiah declared, "All men are like grass, and all their glory is like the flowers of the field. The grass withers and the flowers fall." Then he adds a line of powerful contrast: "But the word of our God stands forever" (Isaiah 40:6-8).

Onto the seemingly hopeless landscape of this bleak world, a blanket of fresh, new snow has fallen. It is no illusion. An infant bearing the banner of hope and the mantle of peace comes with the healing miracle of his forgiveness and love. Here is our hope and the hope of all generations: the innocent babe of Bethlehem, the self-sacrificing God-man dangling lifeless on a cross, the victorious resurrected and ascended Lord interceding at the Father's throne on our behalf. Christ is God's quintessential gift to the ages. Our task is to spread the Good News.

But new and formidable obstacles have been built across the path of God's truth. This generation has experienced enough of the commercial world to know that just about everyone is selling something—a product, a service, an idea, a sensation, a way of life, a religion. Today's young people are skeptics in the extreme; they see through the hype. They are determined to trust no one. Company CEOs, elected politicians, hot babes in TV ads, soft-spoken professors, network news anchors, trusted physicians, wise parents, and even much respected preachers are all assumed to spin their rhetoric in favor of some agenda. They are expected, in fact, to pitch their "product." It's their job.

Within this environment, reaching out to the younger generation is particularly difficult. The gospel message itself may go completely unchallenged, but because the messenger is under suspicion, the message (priceless as it is) may be dismissed out of hand.

In addition, tolerance is touted as being one of our highest values. People in our culture go to extreme lengths not to offend—to be PC (politically correct). On the whole, we Americans see ourselves as tolerant of race, ethnicity, gender, lifestyle, and especially religion. This truly is the *Whatever Generation*. A serious discussion about faith in Jesus is likely to go something like this: "You tell me your faith in Jesus is vitally important to you. Great! I couldn't be happier for you. I find truth and meaning in aroma therapy."

In tandem, cynicism and tolerance represent a formidable barrier to evangelizing the world. And these challenges extend into our own families. Our children, remember, are growing up in a world immersed in cynicism and tolerance. This is hardly the time to shrink back from the opportunities we have to communicate our faith to them.

The congregation in Rome, you may remember, was a cross section of Roman society. Many members of that congregation didn't have the benefit of a background in the Hebrew Bible. Yet, by the power of God's Holy Spirit, they came to believe in the Hebrew God of redemption and reconciliation. The congregation had fine spiritual leaders and opportunities for reaching more people adrift in a pagan society seemed endless. Sound familiar?

Paul wanted every man, woman, and child to be engaged in evangelical effort. It was good for them. It was good for Christ's kingdom. The fields were ripe for harvesting.

But some apparently held back. They were new to the faith. They lacked confidence in their ability to articulate their beliefs. Handling something as holy as God's Word seemed too great a burden. Maybe they were uneducated or unskilled in communication techniques. Perhaps they were fearful of saying the wrong thing, of speaking false doctrine.

Paul would not allow those fledgling members to hide behind such excuses. "I myself am convinced, my brothers," he wrote, "that you yourselves are full of goodness, complete in knowledge and competent to instruct one another" (Romans 15:14).

To be sure, many of our brothers and sisters in Christ are personally involved in the instruction of others. Many Christian parents, for example, are reinstating the practice of holding daily family devotions in their homes. Others do gospel work in a more public capacity. But too many Christians still linger in the shadows, frozen in fear, reluctant to seize opportunities to tell others about Jesus. That must change. Today, as much as in any other time in history, we need to overcome that fear. Our children, our neighbors, and our friends all need to know that there is a way out of this maze of confusion. There is a standard of truth. And there is hope: refreshing, eternal hope, which gushes from the spring of living water—God himself. To remain silent is to let cynicism have its way. Our challenge, eerily similar to the challenge of the early Christian church, is to enlist all God's people for real gospel ministry.

To be ready to meet that challenge, we also need to become more deeply attached to God's truth. Saint Paul wrote, "Let the word of Christ dwell in you richly as you teach and admonish one another with all wisdom" (Colossians 3:16). Therein lies the power for sharing the hope of the risen Christ with others. It is God's enduring truth that motivates, empowers, and prepares us to meet the challenges of speaking God's truth to a generation of cynics.

Young people today can be so challenging. It takes a special gift to be able to reach them. Amelia Lockhart has that gift. Amelia has an uncanny ability to know where kids are coming from. She listens.

Amelia's teen Bible classes are unique. Every week, from 8 to 15 seventh, eighth, and ninth graders show up for her "impromptu" discussions. While the laid-back conversations may seem unrehearsed to the kids, Amelia invests anywhere from eight to ten hours preparing for every lesson. But even with such intense preparation, the dialogue can go anywhere. Amelia is ready to respond with Bible truth no matter what topics the kids might want to explore. She is well grounded in Scripture, making a point of setting aside time every day to read the Bible.

What makes Amelia's group so unusual? Only one of the kids is actually a member of the fledgling congregation she serves. The rest have been drawn to her honest, straightforward approach to discussing the real-life issues today's teens struggle with. Homosexuality. Animal rights. Sex and dating. Abortion. Evolution. Amelia has a knack for knowing when kids are simply goofing around, as all kids will, and when they are talking about something that matters deeply to them. She senses the tension. And she remains unflappable when Christian values are challenged and derided.

This strange mix of kids, many of whom view Christianity as little more than a vague concept, makes for some interesting discussions. Many an experienced pastor would have given up on this group long ago. Occasionally some of the questions do drift out of bounds. But Amelia's patience and self-confidence always win the day.

In a discussion about evolution, one of the boys persists in challenging the concept of faith. Some would even say he is antagonistic. He is looking for scientific proof to provide grounds for agreeing or disagreeing with the Bible's account of creation. It doesn't help that a cute seventh-grade girl sits directly across from the young man. He relishes the opportunity to impress her with his mental prowess.

Amelia takes the challenge in stride. She understands the mix of emotions that flood the adolescent psyche. She understands flirting. But she also understands that from little on the young man has been indoctrinated in the false premises of evolution. He's heard those theories promoted in school as fact, and they are probably reinforced at home. He knows the rationale by heart. "Where's the proof?" he demands.

"How exactly would you define faith?" Amelia asks. Her pointed question launches a healthy discussion about the nature of faith. By the end of the discussion, the kids have worked through their understanding of faith as it apprehends God's chronicle of the creation week. Their statement about faith harmonizes well with the definition provided in Hebrews chapter 11, verse 1.

Amelia's strength lies in her genuine concern for young people who have never known the truth. She cares. And they know that she sincerely wants to know what they believe and why, even if what they tell her is an affront to her own faith. She doesn't become defensive when a teenage girl argues that abortions are okay because the world is too overpopulated. A little probing uncovers the fact that three or four of the girl's friends at school have already had abortions. Amelia quickly realizes that there is a real personal issue here. The girl is struggling. If she agrees that abortion is wrong, she will be forced to consider confronting her friends with their sins.

The kids that attend the teen Bible class come from a wide range of backgrounds, but Amelia has found some common threads woven into their belief systems. They are products of homes that have never given much thought to their spiritual lives. Their parents may have an ambiguous sense of what is right and what is wrong. Their moral values are subject to the tug of the prevailing philosophical tides. The kids have all attended secular schools, in which the popular teachings of the day are woven into a tapestry that promotes the theme of tolerance and the save-the-world-by-saving-nature perspective. These kids do not understand Christian doctrine or Christian worship practices. They have little or no background in Bible history. None of them understand what prayer is all about. They may each have a personal creed, but it may have little real substance or connection with God's truth. If you ask them what they believe, their response is likely to be constructed from street mythology and pop slogans. And, in every case, they are searching for something solid, something to give meaning and direction to their young lives. Amelia is always looking for ways to fill that gap with divine truth.

In an age in which it's easy to give up on young people, even in the church, Amelia is not giving up. For her, the struggle is worthwhile. If she is able to reach only one of these kids with the gospel message, the effort will have been worth it.

Be completely humble and gentle; be patient,
bearing with one another in love.

Ephesians 4:2

CHAPTER TEN

Payday

My father joined my uncle in a business partnership in the late forties: a mail-service company. Their business consisted of little more than a used typewriter, an old labeling machine, and a handful of clients. Their first office was a tiny room in a former bakery shop. Because the early years of their fledgling business were difficult ones, our family was just as impoverished as our neighbors. We too were trapped in the inner city.

I knew that we lived from paycheck to paycheck, and I always knew when payday arrived. It meant that one of the five kids in the family might get a new pair of shoes, or maybe we could finally afford to get the broken television fixed. Mother sewed shirts for us. There was never any money for eating out in restaurants or going to the movies or to baseball games. We shopped for secondhand toys, clothes, shoes, baby buggies, beds, rugs, and bikes—most of our belongings were hand-me-downs. We raised vegetables in a little garden next to the tin garage. It was subsistence living, but we were happy. We hoped my father's business would flourish someday, and then our family might be able to afford some of the trappings of success, perhaps even a better home.

My best friend, Joey, lived in the lower flat just next door. Our houses were built so close together that we could reach out windows in our respective houses and join hands. A child of second-generation immigrants, Joey was a year older than I. We considered his older brother, Stan, an honorary member of our little club. Though he was old enough to get a job, he had the heart of a child and was always hanging around anyway.

Joey's sister, Shirl, two or three years older than Joey, had a winning smile and lots of older boyfriends. Since her social calendar was always full, Shirl didn't hang around the house much.

Like ours, Joey's family was very poor. His father spent long hours at his factory job, apparently putting in a lot of overtime. In order to make ends meet, Joey's mother cleaned houses several days a week.

Joey and I would talk about money every now and then. As kids will, we compared notes to get a read on whose family was the poorest, a dubious honor that neither of us wanted to accept.

But payday meant something quite different for Joey's family than it meant for ours. Every Friday in the evening hours, Joey's mom would send Joey and Shirl on a mission to hunt for their father in one of the local taverns. During the winter months, this happened under the cover of darkness. During the summer when the days were long, the two of them suffered the humiliation of having to drag their drunken father down the street in full view of friends and neighbors.

Now, Joey's father was a big, roly-poly man. On some Friday nights, he could barely even walk. Occasionally the three of them would lurch over onto the pavement together. Then it might take Joey and Shirl ten minutes just to get their dad back in an upright position and onto his feet. Often he was unable to control his bladder, and a dark stain would cover the front of his overalls. Sometimes he would hurl abrasive epithets at neighbors. Sometimes he would babble incoherently or bay at the moon.

These weekly missions had to be carefully timed. If Joey and Shirl found their father before he was sufficiently drunk, he would refuse to come home with them. He had a violent temper when he was drinking, which would erupt if their timing wasn't just right. On those occasions a squad car would have to be called and he would be hauled off to jail. Then Joey and Shirl would have hell to pay the next day when he got out of jail.

But, if they waited too long, their father would end up spending the whole paycheck on booze. If he didn't drink it up, he would give it away to his friends. Or someone would roll him for whatever money he had left. Then the family would face another week without their father's income. In a household already beneath the poverty line, losing that income was a brutal body blow.

When I finally understood what was happening, I despised Joey's dad for what he was doing to his family. Joey kept telling everyone what a great guy his dad was. But I couldn't talk with his dad anymore, even when he was sober and wanted to joke about baseball or girls. I was no longer able to give him the respect I felt all adults should have.

Shirl, on the other hand, was clearly hurting. Sometimes, after she had wrestled her father home, I would see her alone on the front porch, crying. The embarrassment must have been unbearable.

One time, when I saw Shirl crying on her front porch, I went over to console her. I told her everything would be all right, though I knew she didn't believe me. I tried to get her to see that her father had some good qualities. But I felt like I was lying.

Shirl didn't want to hear any of it anyway. She hated her father. She said so with those very words: "I hate my father." She said she wished he were dead. I had never heard any kid say that about a parent before. She hated her mother too for making her baby-sit her father whenever he was drunk and for making her go into those filthy taverns where men fondled her with their eyes.

I didn't know what to do. Kids don't have solutions for those kinds of problems. At least this kid didn't. The only thing I could think of was to try to say a prayer with Shirl. This was what the adults in my world would do. After stumbling over my words, something like a prayer finally tumbled out. Shirl said a few words too, and she finally stopped crying. She pulled out a purple rosary from her pocket, and I waited quietly while she recited a "Hail, Mary, full of grace." Then I left, thinking mine was the wealthier family.

Man's greatest need is for reconciliation between himself and his Creator. But most people today concern themselves with more immediate issues: "Just give me a little peace and quiet later in the day to collect my thoughts." "A modest raise in salary would be nice." "Some new carpeting for the living room would make my day." Our generation seems focused even less on the distant past or the cosmic future than preceding generations. *Now* seems to claim all our energy and attention. *The present* seems to be far more urgent and demanding. This generation wants to be satiated *now*. It wants to find gratification in what it does *now*. When the pain of life descends on us, we want relief *now*. We live in a world totally obsessed with the *here and now*.

The here and now mocks and torments and even tortures the hapless lives of many—those who have no choice but to confront pain and sadness every moment of their lives. These are the people for whom life's hard realities stare them in the face every single day. Among them you will find the terminally ill, the chronically lonely, the anxious and fearful, the insufferably poor, the emotionally tattered and torn, the abused, the physically spent, the discarded, and the disenfranchised. They are fragile and broken people. The world is full of them.

To its credit, our society makes a monumental effort to attend to the downtrodden masses in institutional ways: welfare projects, hospices, prisons, social programs, asylums, medical facilities, research grants. The system is far from perfect. But as a nation, and in the main, we do make an effort. We construct safety nets, trying hard not to forget these people. We enact laws that protect the hurting and the helpless. We spend huge sums of money to support them in whatever ways they need to be supported.

Our efforts on behalf of the distressed far surpass those of many past civilizations. Perhaps we have made some positive

123

strides over the centuries. The social progress that has been made cannot be easily dismissed. Our race is far from eliminating disease, injustice, or poverty, but it would be dishonest to suggest that human efforts have been a complete failure. Look around. We are the beneficiaries of some real progress. This is a blessing unique to life in the modern era. Many people do care enough to make personal sacrifices on behalf of those who carry huge burdens in life. America does seem to have a social conscience, though it is admittedly selective in its focus.

But, all too often, the effect of all this on God's people is confusion. Jesus tells Christians to feed the hungry, visit the imprisoned, and share our cloaks. When a news broadcast projects scenes of hurricane damage in tragic proportions, we mumble, "Oh, how sad!" That footage is immediately followed by shots of Red Cross workers, rushed to the scene to distribute food and fresh water. And we quietly think to ourselves, "Hmm. Seems like someone has that situation well covered."

We read with interest about an innovative hospice program for the terminally ill. The new program is well designed and is a remarkable blessing for the families of those who suffer from some of the most painful human tragedies. We thank God for such programs. And we wonder how we too might help the terminally ill die with dignity and grace.

Then we turn our good intentions closer to home. Perhaps our church is looking for someone to help others bear their burdens—homebound members in need of visits; young, single mothers feeling lost and alone; troubled teenagers desperately in need of a friend. We read reports and hear stories about the work that is being done by agencies within our own church body. We resolve to drop a check in the mail the next day.

It's hard to know just where and how we fit into burden-bearing programs these days. Some of us are quick to volunteer when the need arises. There are plenty of relief agencies, including some that fall under the auspices of the church. They all need our dollars so they can continue to do their fine work.

By its very nature, burden bearing is a personal, intimate way of demonstrating love for another human being. The classic Boy's Town image of an older boy with a younger boy draped over his shoulders comes to mind. The caption reads, "He ain't heavy; he's my brother." Many of today's burden-bearing opportunities have lost that intimacy.

The Scripture passages that urge us to be kind, compassionate, and generous with one another imply the kind of human contact that goes beyond merely opening up our wallets for a special offering. Our acts reflect the attitude of our hearts. Our compassionate burden bearing is quite different from the burden bearing undertaken by unbelievers, for our frame of mind is rooted in an understanding of the kindness and mercy our Lord has shown us.

Carrying someone else's burden is at the very heart of Christ's work on earth. He carried our burden of sin. Imagine that! We were his enemies, sworn in our allegiance to Satan and company. Yet, in our stead, he bowed under the full fury of God's terrible justice.

In love, the same Savior extends to each of us the privilege of sharing the burdens of others. And he emboldens us with the knowledge that whenever we flex our muscles to shoulder another's burden, we are serving him. "Whatever you did for one of the least of these brothers of mine," he said, "you did for me" (Matthew 25:40).

Our outlooks on life will change as we begin to carry the burdens of others. Christ's sacrifice for us gave him immeasurable joy (Hebrews 12:2). So it is with us. The harvest of joy that awaits us in sharing someone else's pain is profound.

Burden bearing is, without a doubt, the most overt form of living for one another. When we think about bearing one another's burdens, we imagine rolling up our sleeves and getting to work in a food pantry or filling sandbags along the banks of a mud-swollen river. The mental pictures help us grasp the essence of burden bearing. It is an *act* of love. It is pushing wheel chairs and sitting for long hours holding someone's hand. It is sending cards and e-mailing messages of encouragement. It is running summer camps for retarded children and spending hours counseling those fragile people. It is spending sleepless nights in prayer. But, at its very pinnacle, burden bearing is also an act of sharing encouragement and hope. That often happens more in the words we say than in the things we do.

Those who carry heavy burdens in life are often searching for answers to life's most difficult problems. They are looking for real encouragement, the kind that helps them stand up to the pain or fight back the tears of loneliness. Christians do not only take the time to listen so that we will know where others hurt. We also offer God's most powerful answers to their pain.

The most satisfying answer to human suffering is the sweet message of salvation—the good news of the cross and our unexpected relationship with the bearer of that cross. In Christ Jesus, mankind's burdens are made lighter. He is our brother. He is willing to carry that portion of the load that we ourselves cannot carry.

For the comfort of his followers, Jesus once described the last days of the world in this way:

> Then there will be great distress, unequaled from the beginning of the world until now—and never to be equaled again. If those days had not been cut short, no one would survive, but for the sake of the elect those days will be shortened. (Matthew 24:21,22)

Did I say Jesus uttered these words for our comfort? This is hardly an optimistic view of the future. If it were not for those last few comforting words of promise, we would most certainly despair over Jesus' pronouncement concerning the last days.

Are we living in those days? Is this the final era in our planet's history? The people of every generation have speculated about the possibility that Jesus was speaking of their age. All things considered, we would be foolish to imagine that he was not speaking of our day. But, as you may recall, Jesus also said that even he didn't know when that day would come. Only his heavenly Father knows that (Matthew 24:36).

We can be grateful that God keeps such information top secret. And we can take heart in the promise that, for the sake of those faithful who are in eternal jeopardy because of their suffering, our all-knowing God will bring an end to all things, sooner rather than later.

The Last Day will come. And as it approaches, life on our planet will become more difficult to bear. For example, we shouldn't be surprised to find ourselves targets of the unbelieving world. Peter encourages those who experience any hardship at the hand of unbelievers with the reminder that God's judgment is about to begin (1 Peter 4:12-19). So we pray even more fervently: "Come, Lord Jesus. Come quickly."

On the other hand, as disturbing as the attitudes of the world may be, perhaps we can also see some positive signs on the horizon. In the years ahead, we may very well face new stresses for the sake of our faith. But it is also quite likely that many new opportunities to build one another up for these challenges will also surface. That was the case for early Christians. Facing martyrdom, their hope in Jesus grew all the more as they comforted one another with God's glorious promises. Today many broken people are searching for real answers to life's most bitter questions. The opportunities to share Jesus with a hurting world are increasing exponentially.

God has placed us into this time and this place for a reason. We are here to preach and teach the story of the crucified and risen Christ to the troubled, the fragile, the lonely, the hopeless. That message offers direction, provides reconciliation, and promises real hope. "Therefore, as we have opportunity, let us do good to all people, especially to those who belong to the family of believers" (Galatians 6:10). And let us "be prepared in season and out of season; correct, rebuke and encourage—with great patience and careful instruction" (2 Timothy 4:2).

When Emily Thompson heard that her neighbors Brett and Rachel were planning on getting married, she was beside herself with happiness. Over the past five years, Emily and Rachel had become very close friends. Emily's husband once observed that the two acted more like sisters than neighbors. They spent many hours together, shopping and just talking.

On several occasions Rachel had shared with Emily her feelings about living together with Brett. It just wasn't enough for

Rachel anymore; she wanted their relationship to be cemented by marriage vows. Now Emily's prayers for the young couple were being answered.

Brett and Rachel were not religious people. At least they weren't religious in the sense that they participated in organized religion. On the other hand, they both held vague convictions about God. They wanted to be good people; they followed some kind of spiritual compass. They searched for answers to their questions about life and the hereafter. They didn't hesitate to become involved in conversations about religion and always respected the beliefs of others. When they finally decided to be married, Rachel thought it would be nice to have a church wedding. Emily planted the idea in Rachel's mind that she should inquire into the possibility of being married at King of Glory Lutheran Church, where Emily and her husband were members.

Rachel liked the idea. She called the church office and quickly found herself talking to Pastor Reimsdorf. He explained that he would be vacationing out of state for a few weeks. Perhaps they could meet and talk a bit before he left. During the course of the conversation, Rachel mentioned that she and Brett were already living together. Pastor Reimsdorf expressed appreciation for her openness.

Brett and Rachel met with Pastor Reimsdorf in his study that same night. The young couple seemed determined to be married at King of Glory. Its ambiance seemed just right for their simple tastes.

After a little small talk to put everyone at ease, Pastor Reimsdorf played a short video that presented law and gospel in very basic terms. The video began by posing the basic spiritual question "If you died tonight . . . ?" Brett, in particular, noted his agreement with the video's powerful message of grace. He told Pastor Reimsdorf his grandfather had been a Lutheran pastor many years ago. Brett had himself been raised as a Lutheran, but he hadn't practiced his faith in more than 15 years. What he had just seen in the video left a strong impression on him. After the couple agreed to return for some additional Bible instruction, the conversation turned to their live-in relationship.

Pastor Reimsdorf told Brett and Rachel that if they believed in God and his promises, they would surely want him to bless their union. That would come through the public declaration of their commitment to each other in marriage. Before they parted, Brett asked when church services were held on Sunday. Though Rachel would be unable to attend because of her job, he would be there.

Pastor Reimsdorf wondered if Brett's enthusiasm didn't seem a bit overplayed, almost melodramatic. The pastor had been disappointed before by the reactions of young people who seemed to view wedding preparation as a sort of social game. He feared that the conversation was following a common pattern: They would show interest just long enough to be married, and then they would never be heard from again. Then again, he wanted to put the best construction on this couple's intentions. One never really knows how or when the seed of faith will take root and begin to grow.

Over the next few days, Pastor Reimsdorf didn't give much thought to Brett and Rachel. Then, on the following Tuesday morning, he received a phone call from Pastor Gibbs, the pastor on call during his vacation. At age 26, Brett had suffered a massive heart attack. He lay in a local hospital in a coma. He was not expected to live. Pastor Gibbs and Rachel had talked at length. They had prayed together, and he had read Scripture passages to Rachel to comfort her. Now Pastor Gibbs was asking for some background on Brett in the event that he would die while Pastor Reimsdorf was still on vacation. Pastor Gibbs was concerned about whether he could, in good conscience, conduct Brett's funeral.

Pastor Reimsdorf remembered the brief confession that Brett had uttered after viewing the video. He also noted Brett's enthusiasm for revisiting the faith of his childhood. There was precious little else to go on to indicate Brett was in the faith when he had suffered the heart attack.

Brett clung to life for another week. By the time he died, Pastor Reimsdorf had returned from his vacation. He was able to conduct the funeral service himself.

Rachel sat in the front row with her mother beside her. Emily Thompson and her husband were there too, as were several of Brett's coworkers.

Pastor Reimsdorf began his sermon by asking the same question that the video presentation had posed: "If you died tonight . . ?" He went on to tell the mourners about Brett's brief confession of faith after seeing the video.

After the committal service, several of Brett's friends remained, talking quietly near the grave. Pastor Reimsdorf introduced himself. Brett's secretary asked Pastor Reimsdorf if Brett had really said the things that were mentioned in the sermon. When Pastor Reimsdorf quoted Brett's words again, the secretary closed her eyes and smiled. "You don't know how happy I am to hear that," she said. "And I need to share something with you."

She then told him that on the day after the couple's visit, Brett had spoken about their meeting. He had told her, "The preacher said it's not right for us to live together, so we're going to move apart until the wedding."

One never really knows when the seed of faith will begin to grow or when it will produce real fruit. We merely sow the seed.

Let us not give up meeting together,
as some are in the habit of doing,
but let us encourage one another —
and all the more as you see
the Day approaching.

Hebrews 10:25

CHAPTER ELEVEN

THE CIVIL DEFENSE MANUAL

In August of 1945—one year before I was born—the United States dropped atomic bombs on the Japanese cities of Nagasaki and Hiroshima. This brought an end to a terrible world war. But it also ushered in a new era of nervous political standoffs and unparalleled potential destruction. This era has been referred to as the Atomic Age. Humanity could now imagine the unthinkable—the possibility of obliterating thousands of years of civilization with the push of a button.

In the early fifties, the Soviet Union became the world's second nuclear power. Communism was seen as a threat to democracy. And with the advent of its own nuclear arsenal, the Soviet Union had also become a serious threat to our national security. With the surprise attack at Pearl Harbor still fresh in America's memory, war readiness ranked high as a national priority.

My father took his civic duty seriously. When a general call went out for civil defense workers who would respond in the public's interest in the event of a nuclear attack, he volunteered. Civil Defense (CD) training sessions were held at the local public school. My father attended the meetings on Saturday mornings and weeknights.

I read the civil defense training manual issued to all CD volunteers. It was filled with detailed traffic patterns, martial law canons, the locations of local bomb shelters, fallout statistics, and graphic scenes depicting the horrors of nuclear war. In my active child's imagination, a worst-scenario holocaust was imminent. According to the manual, Milwaukee was a primary target because it played such a key role in manufacturing and in our country's infrastructure. According to the CD map, our house stood less than two miles from Milwaukee's industrial valley—ground zero.

School administrators were recruited in the national readiness plan. Their job was to prepare teachers and students for the possibility of a daytime nuclear attack. Air raid sirens were installed in every school building. Designated shelter areas were marked with civil defense signs. Children were instructed on what to do in a nuclear emergency. Weekly drills were scheduled. Sirens blared regularly. Jaundiced expressions betrayed our emotions as we were herded into shelter areas. (I harbored a secret plan to escape from school and run the four blocks to our house to die with my own family.)

In the fall of 1962, a series of political events led to a global crisis the likes of which the world had never faced before. The Soviets had managed to parlay their contacts with Cuban leaders into a political toehold in the western hemisphere. According to US intelligence, missile sites had been constructed on the island of Cuba. Soviet medium- and intermediate-range ballistic missiles—each capable of striking the United States with a nuclear warhead 20 or 30 times more powerful than the Hiroshima bomb—were just 90 miles from Miami.

The days that October were particularly beautiful. The air was fresh and clean—good football weather. The sun shone with extra vitality. Larger than usual flights of geese filled the skies. Winter would come early. But the streets, playgrounds, and green markets of our neighborhood were empty.

President John F. Kennedy appeared on national television to address the American public. He spoke with reassuring confidence. This was the kind of nuclear crisis everyone feared. The United States, he explained, was responding to the Soviet threat by placing a naval blockade around Cuba. Its purpose was to keep Soviet ships from delivering their nuclear arsenal. Nuclear war seemed inevitable. We understood that the United States could not afford to let the Soviets gain such an important strategic advantage. But it was the idea of living at ground zero that brought the crisis into sharp focus. Our lives hung in the balance. The world held its breath for the next 48 hours.

My brother and I went outside to toss a football around, but our interest quickly evaporated. Mother and Father washed windows together, their conversation subdued, tense. We tried not to think about the *what ifs*. Instead, we each withdrew to a lonely, private world of fear. There we remained, grieving over the impending night of nuclear horror. There was nothing else to do.

Finally, my mother opened her Bible and told the rest of us to stop what we were doing. She began to read, "The LORD is my shepherd; I shall not want. . . ." Slowly the sun poured its radiant energy into the room. "Yea, though I walk through the valley of the shadow of death," she continued, "I will fear no evil; for thou art with me; thy rod and thy staff they comfort me." Anyone close to ground zero was traveling through the psalmist's dreaded valley that very moment. But the Good Shepherd was there too. He has promised to hold us up in such anxious times. My mother's voice was strong; her words gave us the courage to live each passing minute with new hope. "Thou preparest a table before me in the presence of mine enemies: thou anointest my head with oil; my cup runneth over. Surely goodness and mercy shall follow me all the days of my life: and I will dwell in the house of the LORD for ever" (Psalm 23 KJV).

Our burden had been lifted; we were ready. ICBMs could come raining down on us; we had hope. All was well!

We stand on the brink of an extraordinary age. Actually we are standing, not so much on the brink, but smack in it. When pressed to attach a date to the philosophical metamorphosis that has swept our land, historians point to a time fixed somewhere in the late sixties or early seventies. That's 30-some years ago. The fact is, we are already well into this revolutionary era and have been for some time. And there's nothing we can do to step away from it or turn back the clock. We can perhaps deny it until someone points out that we have been living with our heads stuck in the sand. We can protest, throw temper tantrums, and try to tell the world how foolish it is. As Christians, we are conscience bound to resist and oppose some of the premises of the prevailing philosophy. But most of us have already come to recognize this *new age* as a fact of life. We may even unwittingly contribute to its momentum. Short of packing ourselves and our families off to some mountaintop monastery, there's no way to avoid it. And there's one more fact that every Christian should already know but which certainly bears repeating: the journey of Christians of every generation has taken them through godless terrain. That's a fact. So, what else is new?

Today's world represents an era of unprecedented change. Change that we will need to come to grips with. These are not the normal changes we had come to expect as the torch passed from one generation to the next. These changes are monu-mental—the kind of changes that come along only once every few centuries—changes of epic proportions. Dramatic changes of this kind can undermine one's confidence. These changes are so powerful they are able to paralyze us and sap our life's energy. They affect not only our behavior but the way we think. And yes, they affect even our most personal, deep-seated convictions.

In the preceding pages, we have discussed the cynical view-point that prevails today and the (our) propensity for tolerance. We have considered the way our culture distorts truth, choos-ing instead to devalue absolutes and judge *truth* by the circum-stances of the moment. We've hinted at the trend toward a tribal society and the growing interest in cults. We've addressed the growing lawlessness of our culture. We've taken a look at some of the trends toward New Age mysticism and the occult. And we've discussed the tragic cynical view that dream-ing of a better future is futile. Is it any wonder that so many of our young people have given up their hope? For those who can see only the future's dark side, there is no point to life. Should any of us wonder why the philosophy of our age is becoming increasingly nihilistic? Should we be surprised that young people end up dishonoring their parents, despising authority, mistrusting one another, mutilating their bodies, and destroying themselves with drugs and guns? Powerful forces are shaping the way our culture thinks. And, unless the Lord intervenes, these powerful forces can also change us. The Lord Jesus warned, "At that time many will turn away from the faith and will betray and hate each other" (Matthew 24:10). We cannot afford to be overconfident. We dare not be so foolish as to believe that such religious defection could not happen to us.

To second-generation Christians who had not seen Jesus in the flesh, the apostle John wrote, "We proclaim to you what we have seen and heard, so that you also may have fellowship with us. . . . We write this to make our joy complete" (1 John 1:3,4). John wrote these words to a generation of skeptics—a generation vulnerable to any new idea that came down the pike. Perhaps it all sounded too good to be true—God leaving heaven and coming to this wretched earth in human form. Of Jesus' little band of 12 followers, John was the last living eyewitness. His words bear testimony to the truth of it all. And this is his message: Jesus, the divine Son of God, really lived. John knew the truth of that message. He saw Jesus with his own eyes. He touched Jesus with his own hands. He stood at the foot of the cross with Jesus' mother at his side. He watched the Savior sigh his final breath. But John also saw the empty tomb on Easter morning, and he was on the Mount of Olives to witness his Lord's glorious ascent into heaven. John was there. He spoke the truth.

But things in John's time had changed too. There was a new generation. It needed to hear the gospel too. New doubts had been planted among God's people—tares among the wheat. That generation had its own perspective on history. It had its own understanding of the universe. John wanted that generation to know that what had been said and written about Jesus in the gospels was not a distortion of the truth. Christ Jesus is the real thing—God-man—Savior of the world for all times and for all people.

When he ascended into heaven, Jesus left his followers behind to do the work of spreading the Word to all the nations of the world. Through us, he is still touching the people of that world. His Word lives in our hearts and flows from our lips. His compassionate forgiveness and mercy live in our actions and behaviors. We too proclaim what we have seen and heard in the miracle of God's love for us. We also testify to the mysteries of this faith. We testify to it in our words. And we live our testimony through our actions, attitudes, and behaviors. And those two components of our testimony, our words and actions, are joined at the heart. If preaching is all we do, our words will ring hollow. We are here also to give credence to that message with our actions. That is our joy. And that joy is not stifled by the cynicism of the day.

All hope for sharing the gospel with others is not lost. As cynical, skeptical, and nihilistic as people may be, they retain some basic spiritual instincts. First, there is a desire for something that can never be found in the world. The 20th-century author C. S. Lewis wrote of the longing for the mysterious, the wonderful, the otherworldly that our daily experience does not satisfy. The 17th-century theologian Blaise Pascal called it the God-shaped void in the human soul. And Saint Augustine in the first century spoke of the restlessness of our hearts that could only be satisfied by God. Furthermore, the Bible tells us that a faint shadow of conscience still lingers in the human psyche. There is clearly a primitive fascination with ritual worship, prayer, and the search for some kind of redemption. These instincts still haunt the twisted imaginations of our generation, as does a very real and observable curiosity about our origins. People are desperate to find purpose and meaning in life. They are no different than the men and women of any other age in their fear of death and their fixation on the afterlife.

Because these innate human instincts cannot be easily dismissed, we can be optimistic about reaching out to this generation with real hope. A renewed interest in the supernatural (witchcraft, sorcery, spells, curses, crystals, fetishes, amulets, demons, spirits, sylphs, gremlins, fairies, trolls, ogres, telepathy, myths, and more) opens up interesting new possibilities. There is a desire to believe in something supernatural and mystical. Talk with young people today, and you will hear hints of this desire. The hints are in their vocabulary, in their games, in the books they read and the films and videos they view. That desire is reflected in their music and in the clothing and jewelry they wear. They believe in something quite vague (and certainly not Christian). Some of their beliefs seem to come right out of medieval superstition.[5] Some are connected to technology and have futuristic overtones. There is a desire to believe in something supernatural and mystical. They simply have nothing else to which they can cling.

Christians believe in a virgin birth. We confess our faith in a bodily resurrection. Talk about supernatural! Can you imagine anything more irrational? Have you ever heard of anything as mystical as the Lord's Supper, a sacrament in which Christ

142

himself comes to us physically in his own body and blood, actually present in simple bread and wine? These are awesome mysteries. You and I take them for granted. But they represent an opportunity for sharing Jesus with anyone who has rejected modern logic and reason.

As our culture slowly (or quickly) implodes under the strain of popular dogma, peace will become a rarity. But you and I know the way to everlasting peace. It is based on our hope in Jesus' own sure words of promise. Our most vital *one another* mission is to tell this generation about the forgiveness of their sins won for them in Christ's own sacrificial death on the cross. His victory is their victory too. That is our challenge—a challenge that has not really changed since the first century.

Saint Paul brought that challenge into clear focus for the members of the church in Rome with a self-evaluation instrument. This tool, consisting of four simple questions, was designed to make them take a long, hard look at themselves (Romans 10:14,15). The questions were aimed at rekindling the fires within complacent Christians. Paul asked:

- How can they (unbelievers) call on the one they have not believed in? *(They can't)*

- How can they believe in the one of whom they have not heard? *(They can't)*

- How can they hear without someone preaching to them? *(They can't)*

- How can they preach unless they are sent? *(They can't)*

Paul's challenging questions are still valid today. We Christians of the 21st century would do well to look long and hard into that same mirror. Our fires need to be rekindled with the same sense of urgency. We need to see ourselves filling the important role of sharing the gospel with the people of the world.

That role is not limited to the things we say at home or in church. Our love for a world of lost sinners drives us to penetrate the frontiers of our own safe worlds. Our profession of faith must be clear and strong. And our lives must be consistent with our profession. When people see us loving compassionately in Jesus' name, they will know we belong to him. Some of them will want to know more about our hope, our joy, and our peace. We need to be ready to tell them about the source of all these marvelous blessings that we enjoy in Jesus' name.

We stand on the brink of an extraordinary age—an age not unlike the age Paul and Timothy saw. Consider the solemn charge the apostle gave to his young protege regarding the age in which they lived and the work they had been sent to do:

> In the presence of God and of Christ Jesus, who will judge the living and the dead, and in view of his appearing and his kingdom, I give you this charge: Preach the Word; be prepared in season and out of season; correct, rebuke and encourage—with great patience and careful instruction. For the time will come when men will not put up with sound doctrine. Instead, to suit their own desires, they will gather around them a great number of teachers to say what their itching ears want to hear. They will turn their ears away from the truth and turn aside to myths. But you, keep your head in all situations, endure hardship, do the work of an evangelist, discharge all the duties of your ministry. (2 Timothy 4:1-5)

The evening had not gotten off to a good start. Cumulonimbus rolled in from the northwest. Lightening perforated the slate-colored horizon. Board members, publishing executives, editors, church dignitaries, and their spouses had gathered for an evening of regaling outgoing board members. The entourage was scheduled for a two-hour dinner cruise aboard the *Edelweiss*.

The *Edelweiss* is a restaurant yacht with a reputation for serving excellent food while gliding serenely along Milwaukee's Lake Michigan shoreline. This night, however, promised to be anything but serene. Rain cascaded down the boat's large picture windows. Angry whitecaps reached from the depths. Thunder cracked nearby. Belowdecks we were dry but nervous.

We seated ourselves at linen-covered tables decorated with fresh flowers. "Cocktails, anyone?" The *Edelweiss* motored downriver in spite of the awful weather.

The Hoan Bridge is the last one that boats pass under on their way out into open water. When it was built, the Hoan was to have been linked to a freeway leading to Milwaukee's south side. But because funding had been delayed, for many years the elegantly arched bridge terminated on Carferry Drive—not even close to a major thoroughfare. Locals had affectionately dubbed it the Bridge-To-Nowhere.

As the *Edelweiss* approached the bridge, a cluster of flashing lights at the summit caught our attention—squad cars. Coastguard boats circled in the waters below. Stripped to the waist, a young, brown-skinned man was threatening to jump. He flailed his arms and leaned out over the dark water below.

It was hard to know how to react. Our food had just arrived—Cornish hen, prime rib, Salisbury steak, "Coffee, sir?"—but a life-and-death drama played itself out just a hundred feet above us. Someone at our table tried to relieve the tension with a joke. It wasn't appropriate. It wasn't inappropriate either.

As we passed beneath it, the bridge structure blocked our view of the man. Within seconds the whole awful scene was obscured by a heavy fog, as though a curtain had been drawn before the final scene was over. The incident—at least our view of it—was over just as quickly as it had begun. We were bystanders—observers of just another one of a myriad of gut-wrenching encounters of the human race. Perhaps we were among the last to know this pathetic man or, at least, among the last to know *of him.*

Life at our table on board the *Edelweiss* quickly returned to normal. We ate. We laughed. Those who had witnessed the incident didn't talk about it with the others.

Later that night I lay awake, troubled by the incident. I couldn't erase the picture of the man from my memory. How many others like him were there in the world, people flailing away at the wind on a bridge to nowhere, desperately in need of the hope we take so much for granted? A sense of inadequacy and helplessness covered me like a shroud.

I prayed. It was an afterthought. I prayed for myself. I wanted to ask God to let me sleep—to help me forget the man—to help me forget my inadequacies. But I prayed instead for more compassion, more urgency, more devotion to those who are hurting . . . and dying without hope. I prayed for more opportunities to reach out to the millions whose lives still hang precariously suspended between heaven and hell. I prayed for the man on the Bridge-To-Nowhere, hoping I was not too late in asking God to give him another chance. And I prayed for another chance, for myself . . . and for my church.

AFTERWORD

Every good story begs for closure. In real life, however, we
don't always get to see how our words and actions affect the
lives of others. The Lord has reserved that revelation for
heaven, where nothing will be able to diminish the joy of knowing the whole story. For now we can be content, knowing that
the eternal good that our Lord Jesus seeks for us is the only
closure we will ever need. Still, for the sake of satisfying the
reader's curiosity, I've attempted to tie up a few loose ends.
What I know, I am willing to share.

My father was called to his eternal home in January of 2001.
He was more than ready. He had looked forward to that day for
all of his 81 years. To the very end, he professed the same
strong faith that had brought him safely home at the end of the
Second World War — *his war*, as he called it. He continues to be
my lifelong hero.

My mother remained steadfastly at his side. During his prolonged illness, she regularly reminded us all that we find our comfort and hope in God's enduring promises. Family and friends alike still learn from her example of love for one another.

Letti continues to serve her Lord Jesus in whatever way she can. We watch and marvel at how God's grace is lived out in the lives of living saints like her.

I've lost all contact with the members of the old Brown Street gang—Joey, Stan, Shirl, Marty, and the others. I recently visited the old neighborhood and recalled the days of my youth. It hasn't changed much in a half century. Life there appears to remain as bleak as ever.

Sergio remains committed to fighting the gangsta mentality on Chicago's near north side. He encourages young people to get out while they still can. At every opportunity he integrates his Christian faith with his strong antigang agenda.

Mary's childhood vision was destined for fulfillment. Music has become her lifelong pursuit, though she might never have been able to imagine just how close her youthful reveries came to mapping out her future.

In Mary's professional life as a Christian elementary school teacher, she teaches the joys of singing to kids of the central city. Several have gone on to successful careers in the performing arts. She also directs her church's adult choir and a handbell choir. There, among the musical leaders of her church, she stresses the vital role they have in leading other Christians to articulate the joys of their salvation through song.

Though she is an accomplished organist today, Mary's greatest joy is living out her childhood dream, for she now serves as the director of the Lutheran Chorale of Milwaukee. Every now and then her real choir sings Handel's masterwork.

At the time of the interview, Kip was scheduled for release in three months. The academy made arrangements for him to live with a family in Milwaukee and to attend Wisconsin Lutheran High School, where he would be a member of the senior class. Then, two days before Kip was scheduled to graduate from the Academy's program, the plans blew up again. As of the final edit of this book, Kip is once again living with his father in northern Wisconsin. He has a job in construction work. His future remains uncertain. But his faith in Jesus is firm.

Geraldine and I lost touch after she graduated from grade school. She suffered from kidney failure in her mid-thirties and died in 1979.

When my friend Mick was released from the rehab center, he attended AA meetings faithfully. He also helped others who struggled with similar addictions. About a year later, he thanked me for participating in the intervention.

Each year on the anniversary of the intervention, Mick celebrates his second chance at life. The event resembles a birthday party—alcohol-free, of course. In the years that followed Mick's recovery from alcoholism, his daughters blessed him with more grandchildren. He became a leader in his local parish, devoting much of his retirement time and energy to serving his Lord through the church.

Mick and Myra remain our dear and valued friends.

At the end of the school year, it became necessary to relocate several of Coretta-Jean's grandchildren to new families. Lynetta, the youngest, was permanently placed in foster care with a loving Christian couple. Lauronda has never been moved and will soon be adopted.

During that same year, Chenise became pregnant. Complications to her pregnancy almost took her life. When Corey came to visit his older sister in the hospital, she told him, "Don't ever give the Dumonts a hard time; they're your only family now."

Corey has chosen not to be adopted and has since gone to live with another family. Against the advice of his surrogate parents, he is determined to maintain close ties with his biological mother and some of his aunts and uncles.

The members of Immanuel Lutheran Church continue to keep the six children in their corporate prayers. And for the members, there is still a strong sense that "it sometimes takes a church to raise a child."

Mr. Heisel kept his promise. Following instruction, he was baptized and became a confirmed member of our church. On Sunday mornings you could generally find him attending the early worship service with his wife and Eric.

Because of several changes in my own life, I lost track of Eric and his family. Ten years later in the spring of 1998, I saw Eric on a street corner, waiting for a bus. He had, of course, become an adult and had grown a beard, but I recognized him immediately. I stopped; we chatted briefly. He gave me a phone number. I called and invited him to worship with me on Palm Sunday. He did. We had lunch together and talked about a lot of things, including his spiritual life. He told me he had fallen away from the church. So had his parents. We agreed to meet at church again on Easter Sunday. He never showed up. After that I was unable to reestablish contact. I am still hoping to connect with Eric and his mother and stepfather again.

Cross Lutheran Church on 16th and Vine continues to serve the people of the inner city with distinction, as it did in the days of my youth.[6] Today it has a membership of approximately eight hundred communicant members. While the congregation no longer operates an elementary school, its outreach and community programs have touched many lives and have been fashioned into a highly visible platform from which the gospel is proclaimed. Among the programs are a nationally recognized youth choir, a ministry for reintegrating prisoners into the mainstream community, a youth support program for kids who live with addicted family members, a job placement program for people who have struggled with addiction, and a senior center that specializes in facilitating intergenerational dialogue.

On February 2, 1995, a fire nearly destroyed the church, leaving behind a brick shell of the former edifice. In one year the members found their strength in God to rebuild and restore the half-century-old building. Today the reconstructed church stands as a memorial to all the men and women who committed themselves to the task of bringing the crucified and risen Christ to the people of Milwaukee's near north side.

On the day after the incident on the Hoan Bridge, I inquired at our local police station about the man who was threatening to jump. A spokesperson informed me that the man did indeed jump. But he somehow became entangled on a cable. Police were able to reach him and bring him to safety. I occasionally remember to include the man in my prayers.

Less than a year after that event, the Bridge-To-Nowhere became a bridge to somewhere, as several miles were added to the freeway system. For me it now stands as a symbol of the work that awaits us in these final days of our planet. Our mission is to lead those who have all but given up their hope for a meaningful future to Jesus, their bridge to heaven.

My life, like yours, has been shaped by wars. For whatever battles are still to come during our lifetimes, the Lord is faithful; he will strengthen and uphold us. Often he answers our prayers by giving us Christian friends and family to "one another" us along the way. The wonder of it all is that he also gives us (fragile, weak, trembling cowards that we are) the privilege of reaching out to a world shrouded in darkness. "But God chose the foolish things of the world to shame the wise; God chose the weak things of the world to shame the strong" (1 Corinthians 1:27). We can find joy and delight in the fact that we are among those chosen to do God's will. It is now our turn to cast our bread upon the water.

FOR FURTHER READING

Allen, Ronald B. *The Wonder of Worship: A New Understanding of the Worship Experience.* Nashville: Word Publishing, 2001.

Bernstein, Peter L. *Against the Gods: The Remarkable Story of Risk.* New York: John Wiley and Sons, Inc., 1998.

Bosch, David J. *Believing in the Future: Toward a Missiology of Western Culture.* Harrisburg: Trinity Press International, 1995.

Carson, D. A., general editor. *Telling the Truth: Evangelizing Postmoderns.* Grand Rapids: Zondervan Publishing House, 2000.

Grenz, Stanley J. *A Primer on Postmodernism.* Ann Arbor: Wm. B. Eerdmans Publishing Company, 1996.

Kalergis, Mary Motely. *Seen and Heard: Teenagers Talk about Their Lives.* New York: Stewart, Taboi & Chang, Inc., 1998.

Kundera, Milan. *The Unbearable Lightness of Being.* New York: HarperCollins Publishers, Inc., 1999.

Lakeland, Paul. *Postmodernity: Christian Identity in a Fragmented Age.* Minneapolis: Fortress Press, 1997.

Long, Jimmy. *Generating Hope: A Strategy for Reaching the Postmodern Generation.* Downers Grove: InterVarsity Press, 1997.

Manuge, Dr. Angus, general editor. *Christ and Culture in Dialogue: Constructive Themes and Practical Applications.* St. Louis: Concordia Publishing House, 1999.

Oliver, Martyn. *History of Philosophy.* New York: Barnes & Noble Books, 1999.

Ridley, Matt. *Genome: The Autobiography of a Species in 23 Chapters.* New York: HarperCollins Publishers, 1999.

Robinson, Jenefer, editor. *Music and Meaning.* Ithaca: Cornell University Press, 1997.

Scheiber, Andrea Lee, editor. *What NeXt? Connecting Your Ministry with the Generation Formerly Known as X.* Minneapolis: Augsburg Fortress Publishing, 1999.

Slaughter, Michael. *Spiritual Entrepreneurs: Six Principles for Risking Renewal.* Nashville: Abingdon Press, 1995.

Storr, Anthony. *Music and the Mind.* New York: Ballantine Books, 1992.

Van Doren, Charles. *A History of Knowledge: Past, Present, and Future.* New York: Random House, 1991.

Veith, Gene Edward. *Postmodern Times: A Christian Guide to Contemporary Thought and Culture.* Wheaton, Illinois: Crossway Books, 1994.

Veith, Gene Edward. *Modern Fascism: Liquidating the Judeo-Christian Worldview.* St. Louis: Concordia Publishing House, 1993.

Webber, Robert E. *Ancient-Future Faith: Rethinking Evangelicalism for a Postmodern World.* Grand Rapids: Baker Books, 1999.

Zacharias, Ravi. *Deliver Us from Evil: Restoring the Soul in a Disintegrating Culture.* Dallas: Word Publishing, 1996.

ENDNOTES

[1] The apostle Paul urged the Christians at Corinth to greet one another with a holy kiss (1 Corinthians 16:20; 2 Corinthians 13:12). Scholars do not agree on the nature of such holy kissing. However, we can conclude that such a kiss was a sign of genuine agape love. Contemporary Christians would do well to remember that God blesses us by merely bringing us together. A casual hug, a handshake, and a warm embrace communicate our affection for one another.

[2] For the remainder of this essay, the term *music* refers to everything that's involved in musical expression apart from the text. What we say to one another is the heart of speaking to one another in psalms, hymns, and spiritual songs. It involves our doctrinal teachings. But the way we say it, the musical styles we use as vehicles for our speaking, is equally important. This chapter focuses on the musical styles we can appropriate into our worship choices.

[3] The record actually shows that, during a period of several weeks in August and September of 1963, more than 60 people were baptized at Cross Evangelical Lutheran Church. However, the practice of baptizing en masse began during the late fifties. The author is probably recalling one of those earlier occasions.

[4] Stanley J. Grenz, *A Primer on Postmodernism*, (Ann Arbor: Wm. J. Eerdmans Publishing Company, 1996).

[5] One popular teen subculture identifies itself as being "Gothic." One dictionary definition of *Gothic* includes the idea of something barbaric and medieval. It goes on to describe an atmosphere characterized by "the grotesque, the macabre, or the fantastic," and it also "features irrationality, horror, gloom, desolation, violence, and decadence."

[6] Formerly a member of the Lutheran Church-Missouri Synod, Cross Lutheran Church became a member of the Evangelical Lutheran Church in America in 1976.